The Risk Takers

BY ALEXANDER ROSS

A Financial Post/Macmillan book

Maclean-Hunter Limited

ISBN 0-88896-028-X
Casebound edition

ISBN 0-88896-029-8
Paperback edition

Printed and bound in Canada

For Alec

CONTENTS

ACKNOWLEDGMENTS

Many people helped in the preparation of this book. Christopher Maule and Isaiah Litvak of Carleton University first suggested the idea of a book on Canadian entrepreneurs. In fact, we originally planned on doing it together, but sabbaticals and other projects intervened. Just the same, their research and encouragement were invaluable.

The federal Department of Industry, Trade and Commerce, which has an interest in promoting technological entrepreneurship, also helped — not only financially, but by providing information and leads on companies that couldn't have been obtained elsewhere. Alan Vanterpool, Frank Doyle and John Vincent of ITC's Office of Science and Technology were especially patient and helpful.

The heroes of this book, the people it's about, were most helpful of all. All of them are hard-pressed and extremely busy; but all of them gave me as much time and frankness as I needed. So thanks are in order to Dave Hazlewood, Russ Benson, Don and Ron Southern, Phil Japp, Wilson Southam, Ian Bruce, Charles Leblanc and Laurent Beaudoin. Without them, there'd be no book. Without people like them, this country would be much more of an industrial backwater than it is.

Finally, thanks to Paul Deacon and Neville Nankivell at The Financial Post who taught me a lot about business when I was working there and later encouraged me to do the book; and to Bob Perry of The Post and Doug Gibson of Macmillan of Canada, who not only handled the manuscript, but waited patiently for it to arrive.

Special thanks: R. M. Knight, Mary H. E. Atkinson, Murray Sinclair, Ben Webster, John Hardie, Linda Rosenbaum, Moses Znaimer, Nick Steed, J. J. Brown, Norman Short and Michael de Pencier.

"Being good in business is the most fascinating kind of art. During the hippie era people put down the idea of business — they'd say, 'Money is bad,' and 'Working is bad,' but making money is art and working is art and good business is the best art."

Andy Warhol

WHY PEOPLE TAKE RISKS

My friends Dick and Murray had rescued their gold mine from bankruptcy that very afternoon, and now they were drinking downtown in Toronto, reliving the day like tennis players after a hard match. The lawyers and accountants were still sitting around a board-room table in a trust company in Montreal, handing pieces of paper back and forth. But the deal they'd put together was firm, and the closing in Montreal was only a formality, a ritual conducted by the tidy-minded. After two months of scrambling for money, Murray and Dick had made a deal with another company that would guarantee them enough cash to bring their mine into production. It had been a near thing. The mine employed several dozen miners, who were digging the ore out of the ground. Dick and Murray needed additional financing to buy the mill equipment that would convert those large piles of rock into money. They couldn't lay anybody off; once a new mine does that, it loses credibility and can never again attract good miners. So Dick and Murray, for the past two months, had been staggering from payroll to payroll. Some weeks they'd get interim financing from a bank. On two occasions, they'd pledged their *personal* bank accounts to meet the payroll. For several weeks, in other words, they'd been facing the imminent possibility of sudden bankruptcy —the loss of car, cottage, credit cards, bank balance, everything.

What impressed me about these two men, as we sat around a tavern table cracking peanuts and knocking back round after round of drinks, was that neither of them regarded their experience as extraordinary. This was *normal* for them, the experience of knowing that tomorrow you might be wiped out. It was the sort of uncertainty that would produce unbearable stress in most people. For Dick and Murray, it was simply an environment they inhabited.

Later that evening, after many drinks, we got talking about why they did it. What made them live this way? Was it the money? "No," said Murray, "because being up and being down feels about the same." He'd dropped at least a million on paper on the market in the last couple of years. But he still wore the same clothes, drove the same car, lived the same way. So it couldn't be the money. Well, was it the joy of the game itself? Dick used to be a big-game hunter — he'd once been on safari with Hemingway, no kidding — and, yes, he could see certain similarities between the imminent prospect of a bankruptcy order and facing a charging elephant.

And then somebody made a heavy suggestion. "What you guys are doing," said one of their friends, "is trying to defeat death. You're trying to build monuments that'll stay around longer than you do." Dick looked into his drink and thought about that one. In fact, he didn't sleep much that night, because he kept thinking about it after the party was over. But Murray had the last word. "It's not about death and it's not about monuments," he said. "It's about living — living to the hilt." Murray looked into his drink too, and then brightened. "You know," he said, "I enjoy everything I do. Everything!"

Another vignette: I am sitting in a Vancouver living room, drinking scotch with one of the classic Canadian entrepreneurs — a man who'd put together what is now one of Canada's biggest energy conglomerates. He made deals and raced sailboats and made friends with a quality of — well, there was something very *graceful* about the way he did all those things. But on the night in question, he was that saddest of spectacles: the promoter without a deal. A few things had gone sour in his life. And now he'd have lunch with his cronies at the club most days, and spend time in the office most afternoons. He kept looking at various deals, but nothing felt quite right. The truth is, he'd always been a lucky man, and now he wasn't lucky any more. Things weren't connecting in that old sweet way, and now he had an unaccustomed amount of time on his hands.

And so, whenever I came back to my home town for a visit, we'd get together and talk. He did most of the talking, actually, and I listened. There is one night I especially wish to remember. He was talking about the opportunity for an integrated northern transportation company — bush planes, river barges, trucks, railroads, everything that moved. I couldn't reproduce what he said, but the recollection of that long monologue is beautiful. As he talked, you could *see* the thing unfolding: companies being formed, mergers clicking into place, tracks and pipelines being pushed across the tundra, freight rates dropping to the point where one of the planet's largest, richest, least inhabited tracts of territory became accessible to the pride and plunder of corporate man. He had a financier's mind, which does not mean, as is commonly supposed, that he thought purely in terms of numbers. There was nothing dry and statistical about this discourse, because my friend, spinning that vast corporate web in his mind, was giving expression to what I've come to regard as one of the purest facets of the human imagination: something I call the entrepreneurial leap.

You see, in his life and on that particular evening, my friend was really doing what artists do: creating something where nothing had existed before. There is a great deal that is grubby and futile and humanly destructive about business. But to me there is nothing ignoble about this basic entrepreneurial impulse, because it lies very close to my notion of what human beings are all about.

In every aspect of human affairs, from building button factories to achieving nirvana, growth necessitates risk. And this risk-taking impulse, this rare human capacity to make the next jump outward into the unknown, has something of the divine about it.

I'm perfectly aware that the end result of this existential impulse might be a factory that belches sulphur all over the landscape and exploits and cripples its workers in order to produce something silly or harmful, and to make a few coupon-clipping widows neurotically rich. On the other hand, it could be some-

3

thing as mundanely beneficial as a machine that squashes up garbage more efficiently than its predecessors. Whether the end result is wholesome or appalling, you have to respect the original impulse that created it.

What I'm trying to do in this book is observe that impulse in action. I've looked at seven companies in various parts of the country. Each of them started as a gleam in somebody's eye a number of years ago. Today, some of those companies are corporate giants; others are still finding it dicey to meet next week's payroll. All were started by men who share certain characteristics. They are dreamers — which doesn't mean they're impractical; only that they're capable of imagining futures that can be shaped by their own efforts and dreams. They are hard workers; in some instances neurotically hard workers. But to the entrepreneurs in this book, all those 16-hour days don't seem like "work," which is something unsatisfying that you perform largely for the benefit of somebody else. As with artists, their "work" and their lives have assumed a sort of seamless unity, so that what they do and what they are become indistinguishable.

Not all of them are rich. Some will leave estates worth tens of millions; others could die broke. None of them, interestingly, is in it for the money, although they concede that money is a splendid way of keeping score. But money wasn't their basic motivation.

Freedom, not wealth, is their goal — the itch to build something of their own. Most of these men, before they took their first entrepreneurial leap, had reached a point where they were somehow frustrated; they knew they had potential that wasn't being used.

There's one more characteristic that most of the entrepreneurs in this book share: a very direct, intimate relationship with *things*. They're all tinkerers, the rare sort of man who can design a machine, or a process, that will do a job better than it's been done before. This was a deliberate choice on my part, for two reasons. Technological entrepreneurship — the process of developing new products that will sell — is probably the most intensively creative form of entrepreneurship. It also happens to be the kind of entrepreneurship that this country most desperately needs. Canada is probably the world's richest underdeveloped country. We live well by selling our resources to outsiders. We are not primarily a

manufacturing country; and until we become one, we will probably remain the world's best-paid colony.

Any long-term strategy for national survival has to include an
emphasis on manufacturing. The existence of a strong manufacturing sector in a country's economy is evidence that a nation has,
literally, learned how to *use* its brains. In Canada, there exists
what amounts to an organized conspiracy *against* manufacturing.
The men in this book, accordingly, have all struggled against economic odds that are stacked unnecessarily heavily against them.
In fact, I would say that any individual who tries to start a manufacturing business in Canada today must be some kind of nut; the
odds against success are daunting, and he could probably earn a
better return on his money by putting it in the bank.

Still, new businesses happen. The ideas are too good; the
energy level is too high; that old entrepreneurial dream of building something of one's own is too urgent to be denied. So all the
men in this book and the businesses they created strike me as
slightly miraculous. There was a beautiful moment in the summer
of 1973 when Dave Hazlewood, the Vancouver engineer who'd
been living on hamburger and hope for years, while he tried to
develop the first Canadian light aircraft in a generation, stood on
a hill beside the runway and watched his dream roll down the tarmac and, for the first time, lift off into the blue air. There's always
something mysterious and magical about an airplance taking off.
But for me, there was something almost awesome about the fact
that the dreams and energies and skills and persistence of a few
men had put that airplane into the air.

So it *can* be done. God knows it isn't easy. But there are still
people in this country, lots of them, who are taking ideas and
making them fly. There ought to be more of them. I'm hoping that
these seven case histories of Canadian entrepreneurs will encourage other Canadians to take their own ideas and make them fly.

My old Volkswagen van had been breaking down all across
the American plains — wheel bearings, blowouts, steering, a
brake failure on the freeway, everything — and I was three days
behind schedule. So I picked up a hitch-hiker to help with the

driving. With one man alternately sleeping and one man at the wheel, we rolled nonstop, day and night, through Wyoming, Utah and Nevada. It wasn't until the middle of the Nevada desert, with the sun just starting to lighten the sky behind us, that we both found ourselves awake at the same time and did some talking.

He looked like your standard hitch-hiking hippie and, sure enough, he was engaged in your standard hippie cottage industry back home in Rochester, New York: candle making. "Well," I said politely, "about how many candles did you sell last year?"

"That's the trouble, man," he said. "We grossed $100,000 last year, and it's starting to scare me. So now we've got tax problems; my partner and I are arguing about whether to expand; the New York department stores are screaming for more candles. The good feeling's gone out of it. So I went on the road to think it over."

He wasn't kidding. Beneath that long hair and denim uniform, the man was an honest-to-God entrepreneur. He and his partner had designed a candle sheathed in redwood bark which, he said, gave out a warm, woody glow when you lit the wick. It was a unique product, and it was catching on. They couldn't make the things fast enough. They'd even started in-store promotions: special counter displays in the better department stores, cardboard racks in shopping centre Woolcos. "And I'll tell you something," he said. "When I go into those stores and see those displays, which wouldn't be there except for me, you know what? It *thrills* me. I actually get a thrill out of it. Isn't that absurd?"

He was an interesting man: a member of the counter-culture who found himself, to his own considerable wonderment, participating in the achievement ethic. And enjoying it. He was enjoying it so much it worried him.

Social scientists, mostly in the United States, have made extensive enquiries into the hows and whys of entrepreneurial behavior. Their conclusions, as you might expect, haven't been terribly conclusive. But the questions are fascinating. Why do some countries seem to produce so many entrepreneurs and others so few? Why do entrepreneurs take risks, anyway? And what kind of risks? What is the relationship between entrepreneurship and a

6

nation's economic growth? Why do the economies of some countries spurt ahead, while others stagnate? Is it climate — and, if it is, how do you account for Brazil's astonishing growth rate? Do hierarchical societies reinforce traditional values and thus stifle entrepreneurship and innovation — and, if so, how do you explain Japan? Is it race? Colonialism? Religion? Calvinism, according to some scholars, is supposed to have provided the psychic underpinnings for the rise of capitalism. If so, again, what about Japan? What does nature have to do with it? Do most successful entrepreneurs have weak fathers and authoritarian mothers? Are entrepreneurs sick ego-animals, painfully trying to achieve security by building a world for themselves, their own business, that they can control and understand? Or are they, as Joseph C. Schumpeter insisted, heroic *Übermenschen*, the true movers of a society, impelled by the "desire to found a private dynasty, the will to conquer in a competitive battle, and the joy of creating"?

The questions are endless. Speculating about entrepreneurial behavior, in fact, soon enlarges itself to speculations about society as a whole. But it is the job of social scientists to substitute hard fact for speculation. And among the studies conducted since 1945, there have been several that, although less than wholly conclusive, have at least isolated a few interesting correlations.

Perhaps the most authoritative, and by far the most ambitious, are the studies conducted by David C. McClelland, an American psychologist who dipped into such diverse fields as sociology, ethnology, literature, mythology, psychometrics, statistics and macroeconomics in his attempt to provide a workable answer to the question: why do some economies grow while others stagnate?

McClelland's basic proposition is that some nations, just like some people, are more achievement-oriented than others; and that this level of achievement-need (or *n* achievement, to use his term) can be measured fairly precisely, in people and in whole societies.

This involved two rather basic assumptions: (1) that *n* achievement is usually associated with entrepreneurial behavior; and (2) that if you have a lot of entrepreneurs dashing around launching various enterprises, you get economic growth.

To test this notion, McClelland and his colleagues studied folktales and, for industrialized societies, the stories children read

7

in their primary-school readers. Using an elaborate measuring system, he determined the n-achievement level in these stories which, it was presumed, reflected the dominant values of the culture that produced them. The researchers then compared these results with various indexes of a nation's economic growth, such as electric power production.

It may seem a trifle weird for grown men to be seeking a connection between, say, *Little Red Riding Hood* and the Hoover Dam, but they did get some interesting correlations. They analyzed the foktales of 45 preliterate tribes, and found that the tribes whose oral culture contained tales of heroic deeds against incredible odds tended to be the ones that displayed a significant amount of entrepreneurial activity. "Despite all the obvious flaws in the data," McClelland concluded, "a significant relationship exists between n-achievement level in folktales and presence or absence of full-time entrepreneurial activity in the culture."

There have also been entrepreneurial studies that amounted to mass psychoanalysis. O. F. Collins and D. G. Moore, in a 1964 study of 110 small business establishments in Michigan, drew a portrait of the Entrepreneur as Loser, an exile from conventional business structures, the very antithesis of the successful organization man: "Our study suggests that the 'carriers' of the basic entrepreneurial values of our society tend, paradoxically enough, to be those who are marginal to the established social networks. They are those who, for social, psychological, ethnic, or economic reasons, cannot make a go of it in existing social structures. In their search for new paths, they discover little nooks and crevices within the economic and technological network of our society. Some merely hang there, held by fragile tendrils, but others gouge out a spot for themselves and sit securely."

The entrepreneur, in other words, hasn't so much transcended the corporate bureaucracy as he's been rejected by it: "Certainly the entrepreneur does not have the qualities that would make for success in established organizations. His occupational history [is] spotty and filled with evidence of restlessness and inadequacy in organized settings." The composite personality that emerged from the Collins-Moore study was uncomfortable with authority and unskilled at managerial problem solving. He was an outcast from The Organization; and, as the creator of a business of his own, he certainly wasn't having much *fun*. "No one," wrote Collins and Moore, "would undertake the development of a new business unless he had compelling reasons for doing so. More than this, the compelling reasons are not likely to include the star-spangled, glittering attraction of the entrepreneurial way of life. It is just not that good. Few of our respondents went into business for themselves with any illusions about quick success or riding gloriously to the top in a Cadillac convertible. If they had such dreams, they were soon dispelled. Indeed, the evidence seems to be that they went into business for themselves and stuck with it through thick and thin because they had to; there was no other choice for them."

Well, that's one portrait. A more specialized, and probably more relevant, picture was drawn in 1972 by Professors Christoper Maule and Isaiah Litvak of Carleton University, who intensively interviewed 39 founders of technologically based Canadian manufacturing firms. The personality composite that emerges in this study is drastically different from the Collins-Moore portrait. The subjects of the Collins-Moore study were mostly *small* businessmen, the proprietors of machine shops and laundromats and hardware stores. Maule and Litvak studied a different breed: usually men who had invented something, and had managed to manufacture and market it. It's the difference between generals and foot soldiers, or between novelists and newspapermen. Since technological entrepreneurs are also the subject of this book, I found the Maule-Litvak findings far more consistent with my own impressions of the people I'd been meeting.

Although the average age of the Maule-Litvak entrepreneurs was 47, most of them had started their first company between the ages of 35 and 40. This certainly squares with the experience of the people in this book. It also squares with common sense; before you're psychically strong enough to start your own company, you must usually (a) have acquired sufficient working experience and technological expertise, usually by working for somebody else; and (b) have managed to grow up. It isn't until their 30s that most men fight their way clear of all the "shoulds" that have been laid on them by parents, peers and society, and start doing things their own way. One behavioral psychologist characterizes this tendency as "BOOM" — "becoming one's own man."

The Maule-Litvak subjects also had fairly settled childhoods. Most spent their first 18 years in the same town and had fairly settled religious affiliations. A relatively high proportion of these entrepreneurs, at least those born in Canada, had fathers who worked for themselves — 48 percent of the Canadian-born subjects and 27 percent of the foreign-born. This, too, squares with common sense. The man whose father ran his own business seems less likely to be overawed by the process. In the case of the foreign-born entrepreneurs, only 27 percent of whose fathers were self-employed, "the motivation for becoming self-employed may have come from financial and social constraints which these entrepreneurs experienced as children of parents of a lower socio-economic strata," wrote Maule and Litvak.

Wherever they came from, they managed to get good educations — nearly 60 percent had university degrees — and after graduation they typically moved on to managerial jobs in large corporations. They usually did well at their work and, on the average, switched jobs two or three times before starting their own company. Under the ground rules of the Maule-Litvak study, the subjects were all "successful" entrepreneurs, in the sense that their businesses had managed to survive for several years. But about two thirds of them, interestingly, said they were willing to start another company later on. "It appears that entrepreneurs are seldom satisfied with limiting their business horizons to the establishment of a single firm," the authors observed. "This point is all the more noteworthy since the great majority of the entrepreneurs had already established more than one company at the time the questionnaire was completed."

The popular notion is that innovation occurs in a vacuum: a light bulb magically appears one day above the head of some anointed individual, and a company is born. The Maule-Litvak study, however, indicated a less dramatic process. Typically, the entrepreneur, in the course of his work for a large company, spots some trend or some promising new invention; or spots a gap which he figures out a way to fill. In a large proportion of the cases (83 percent), the entrepreneurs indicated that their former companies would not have allowed them to exploit their ideas. So they struck out on their own. "There appears to be a considerable amount of technology transfer from their former employer's organization," the study said. "In other words, the fledgling entrepreneur usually tried to exploit that which 'he knows best.' "

The typical pattern for Canadian technological entrepreneurs, then, goes something like this: You grow up square, in a stable family environment. You get a technical degree, usually at McGill or University of Toronto. You get a job with a big company; usually in the technical end of the business. You become more of a technical man than a managerial generalist. You switch companies every five years or so, usually graduating to a higher salary and more responsibility. You get very good at a narrow technical specialty. You also grow increasingly dissatisfied with the rigidities of big-company thinking. One day you spot a smart idea, either your own invention or something you encounter in your work. You quit your job and start a company on a shoestring, usually with personal savings and the investment of a small group of investors, often including family and friends. And for most entrepreneurs, that's the beginning of the most intense, most involving experience of their lives.

"Entrepreneur? I think the word itself has a touch of insanity to it, because it typifies a man pursuing his own peculiar lust, usually at the cost of enormous discomfort."

The speaker was Moses Znaimer, a former TV journalist who, with the backing of a group of friends an an imaginative venture-capital firm, had helped start a television station. Now he was managing the place, and it was a madhouse — and, as he spoke, a madhouse that was losing money (although Toronto's CITY-TV later edged into the black). It was nearly midnight. He was sitting at the desk he'd been riding since eight that morning. If, in a year or so, the station became profitable, Moses knew he'd be a hero. If it failed — and, on that particular evening, it didn't seem like an impossibility — he knew there'd be a lot of people who would gloat. He loved his job. It was like mountain climbing:

"It's a very athletic proposition. But what's nice is that it's a calculus that's so existential that you wish all your life were like that. I mean, it's so clear-cut! You have a clear sense of rewards and punishment.

"Sure, there are costs. There's not much of a private life. There's a brutal assault on your own personality. On your body too.

"In fact, that's one of the weird contradictions. Capitalists are supposed to be possessive individualists, right? Well, the only thing an entrepreneur doesn't have a possessive, individualist attitude towards is his own body. And that's peculiar. Your intensity is all directed outwards, towards the organism you're creating. And what you neglect most is the ownership and control of your own housing — the only thing you really have! See, the most extreme capitalists in fact give up themselves. They share communally their body, their health, their peace of mind.

"But that's not my major concern. What bothers me most is something you usually experience in a love affair: the better your relationship is going, the more concerned you become that it won't last. I get such an enormous range of stimulus out of this job, that I've begun to ask myself what on earth I would possibly do if I had to stop doing it. There's nothing I know of that combines the sublime and the ridiculous in such an unending, rapid series of challenges."

Znaimer, you see, was positively reveling in this atmosphere of risk and stress and uncertainty. Not everyone would, of course — which raises the question: What kind of people start companies, and what kind don't? Mary Atkinson attempted to answer it in her MA thesis at the University of Western Ontario in 1972. Using interviews and a battery of psychological tests, she compared the responses of 41 laboratory workers with those of 41 men who used to work in laboratories, but had left to start their own Canadian companies. The average age, intelligence and educatioal background of both groups were approximately the same, but here's how some of their responses differed.

Both groups were given something called the French Insight Test, which tries to measure a person's need for accomplishment by asking him to write open-ended comments on such statements as "Don is always trying something new" or "Tom never joins clubs or social groups." Sure enough, the entrepreneurs, according to this measurement of their drive to succeed, scored higher than the salaried laboratory workers.

Both groups also played a card game that allowed the subject to choose between high- and low-risk strategies. The subject could bet on which color, red or black, would turn up next (here he had a 50-50 chance), or which suit (four to one), or which number (13 to one) and so on. As the game progressed, the subject could alter his strategy in the hopes of winning a dollar from the interviewer. As Ms. Atkinson predicted, the entrepreneurs' risk-taking propensities, as measured by this method, were nearly twice those of the laboratory workers. Another test revealed that the entrepreneurs *perceived* themselves as big risk takers — bigger plungers, in fact, than their actual performance in the card game revealed them to be.

The two groups also performed a "sensation-seeking" test, by checking off statements such as the following: "(a) I think all people who ride motorcycles have an unconscious need to hurt themselves; (b) I would like to drive a motorcycle." As expected, the entrepreneurs again scored higher, on the average, than the lab workers.

Other tests revealed further differences. The entrepreneurs indicated less of a need for affiliation with groups; they were somewhat more aggressive; they attached about the same importance to autonomy; they scored lower on tests that measured harm avoidance, and marginally higher on tests that measured dominance. And they weren't significantly more impulsive than the lab workers. Among Ms. Atkinson's conclusions: "Either the risk involved in starting an enterprise has to be reduced, or the risk-taking level of the technological population and investors in Canada has to rise. Traditional conservatism appears to be the antithesis of successful innovation."

"I went down to my office on Sunday morning," said the musician, "*My* office. Everything was quiet, and I looked around. *My* desk. *My* secretary's desk. *My* adding machine. *My* typewriter . . . Jesus! All those *things* — a whole roomful of things. And I saw how they were tying me down. I'd like to go live in Bavaria for a year and just write music. You know why I probably won't go? It's because of that roomful of things downtown. I started that little company to work for me. But now *I'm* working for all that goddam machinery."

Poor bastard. He's one of Canada's better musicians. Because he's got a large family and a sense of stability, he formed the company to churn out sound tracks for TV commercials. The man is very good at what he does, and of course his company is successful. Making a small killing, in fact. But he's not an entrepreneur. His ego isn't invested in the growth of that little company. His ego and his dreams are somewhere else, way out there flitting among the Bavarian alps. For him, the entrepreneurial life is a swamp of trivia, sucking him deeper and deeper into the humdrum, further and further away from his real aspirations.

This little mosaic I've been assembling in the last few pages is intended to add up to a sort of composite view of the entrepreneurial personality. Social scientists are doing their best to quantify this creature and, as I've tried to show, have at least succeeded in confirming the obvious: that entrepreneurs are hard-working, risk-taking, aggressive, et cetera. But what are they *like*? The whole point of this book is to try to show what they're like, by showing them in action. I haven't got any sweeping conclusions on the entrepreneurial personality. But, after encountering a good number of entrepreneurs, I've learned to expect certain characteristics in their mental makeup.

For one thing, they're determined, almost unbelievably so. I don't think you can overstress the extent to which these men persist in the pursuit of their dreams, against really appalling obstacles. I'd give up. So would you, I bet. But entrepreneurs don't.

When I began researching this book, one of my ground rules was that I'd only look at companies that had "made it" — were out of the woods at least to the extent that I could be reasonably sure they'd still be around when the book was published. That rule turned out to contain a major misconception of what the subject is all about. For the whole point of being an entrepreneur is that you *don't* know if your company's going to be around next

14

year, or even next week. Week after week, year after year, these men live with the most awesome uncertainty: that their whole *raison d'etre* could be wiped out almost instantly — by a shaky bank loan, by an economic downturn, by competition they didn't expect, by the weather, by anything. A company must become very large indeed before it transcends this perilous condition. Once it does get that big, it's usually too large and bureaucratic for the man who founded it. If he's smart he'll move onto something else, or allow himself to be supplanted by a bunch of young MBAs, or die. The company that doesn't live in constant fear of imminent failure, in other words, either isn't going anywhere, or it's already arrived.

This may not be true of all service or retail business. But it's almost always true of manufacturing companies, and it seems to be invariably true, in this country at least, of companies that were founded to exploit some technological innovation.

The world, you see, is hostile to innovation. This may even be a biological inheritance of the human organism, whose brain, in order to make sense of the stimuli presented to it, must organize those stimuli into coherent patterns, and thus resists the introduction of anything that threatens to disrupt those patterns. It isn't enough, in other words, to build a better mousetrap. After it's built, the entrepreneur's work begins: to bully the world into accepting the proposition that it needs a better mousetrap. Somehow, he must persuade the world to share his vision. And this is never easy. My favorite illustration of this comes from a Boston newspaper in 1867, three years before Alexander Graham Bell arrived in Brantford.

"A man about 46 years of age," reads the newspaper clipping, "giving the name of Joshua Coopersmith, has been arrested in New York for attempting to extort funds from ignorant and superstitious people by exhibiting a device which he says will convey the human voice over metallic wires, so that it will be heard by the listener at the other end.

"He calls the instrument a telephone, which is obviously intended to imitate the word 'telegraph,' and win the confidence of those who know of the success of the latter instrument, without understanding the principles on which it is based.

"Well-informed people know that it is impossible to transmit

15

the human voice over wires, as may be done with dots, dashes and signals of the Morse code and that, were it possible to do so, the thing would be of no practical value.

"The authorities who apprehended this criminal are to be congratulated, and it is to be hoped that his punishment will be prompt and fitting, and that it may serve as an example to other conscienceless schemers who would enrich themselves at the expense of their fellow creatures."

Coopersmith, whoever he was, had the vision; but he didn't succeed in selling it to the rest of the world. As I said, it's never easy.

Another characteristic that appears to be shared by all the entrepreneurs I've encountered is their commitment to the innovative process. In this, they really are like artists, or mountain climbers. As Mary Atkinson's study indicated, entrepreneurs are not primarily motivated by a desire for wealth or power, but by a deep-felt need to achieve. And, although most of them will tell you they hope to be handsomely rewarded for their efforts, it's not the payoff that interests them as much as the struggle itself.

This impulse can be expressed in two ways. For an authentic technological genius like Joseph-Armand Bombardier, the motive is to build *things* — in his case, snowmobiles. For another kind of entrepreneur, the motive is to build an organization around the "thing" — to transform the gleam in some inventor's eye into a functioning, profitable company. Both impulses are essentially creative; and both kinds of entrepreneurs, once they've succeeded in their initial goals, are usually anxious to move onto something else. No true entrepreneur picks up his chips and goes home after a winning streak. Almost always, he bets again.

Moses Znaimer, before he helped found his TV station, was a partner in the venture-capital firm that provided most of the start-up funds for the project. "One of the pieces of rhetoric in the venture-capital trade," Znaimer says, "is, when people ask you why you're doing it, you answer: 'I'm doing it to make my own big buck, I want the equity.' Well, the truth is they do what they do regardless of rewards. They're doing it because they're bloody-minded, and they'd do it whether there was a reward at the end or not."

There can, of course, be big rewards. The middle classes love to exchange folktales about people who Made a Killing in the market; Joe bought gold at $35, and now it's $205; or Manny bought Xerox at $2.50, and now it's $300; or Peter bought a house in Rosedale or Shaughnessy, and sold it two years later for a $95,000 profit. What's seldom realized is that the rewards possible in this sort of market exercise — buying something and then selling it for more than you paid — are peanuts compared to the potential financial reward when you create something of your own, then sell some of it to other people.

An entrepreneur, when he founds a company that goes public, usually keeps a healthy chunk of the issued stock for himself. When he starts, it's worth nothing. Frequently, when he's finished, it's still worth nothing. But in those rare cases where the company embodies an idea whose time has come, then the entrepreneur's once-worthless block of stock can be worth millions, even billions.

Securities regulations won't allow promoters to cash in such winnings immediately: they "freeze" the entrepreneur into his stock for a while, to protect the outside shareholders. For that reason and others, the entrepreneur who's riding a successful public company normally hangs on to most of his stake. If the company ever reaches the point where it's delivering reliable profits, he can retire on the dividends. More typically, if the company ever reaches that blissful state, he'll eventually sell out for cash, or for shares in a larger company. That's how entrepreneurial fortunes are made.

But most entrepreneurs don't get rich, and don't really expect to. For instance, Canadian film makers, who exist in a state of chronic capital starvation, are usually content if the film they've just made earns enough money to allow them to make the next one. The final payoff isn't what's important. The creative process is. For most entrepreneurs, all they really want is enough payoff to enable them to continue doing what they're doing. This is a sensible attitude toward the matter of compensation, and it's possessed only by happy men.

One final word on the entrepreneurial personality. As far as I know, this proposition hasn't been tested by the social scientists, but maybe it ought to be: the most successful entrepreneurs seem to be happily married. Most of the men in this book have good marriages with bright women. Indeed, if they didn't, it's hard to see how they could continue to lead the kind of lives they do. None of the marriages was an unequal relationship. The wives weren't submissive little mice who fetched the pipe and slippers each night when Hubby came home from the corporate wars. The wives, in fact, seemed to be partners. They understood the business, and the nature of the challenge, at least as well as their husbands.

Entrepreneurs, almost by definition, are people who choose the path of most resistance. So maybe it's not surprising that so many of those I've met seemed to draw strength from a good relationship with a good woman.

2

WHERE THE MONEY COMES FROM

For years I've been hearing the same scenario over and over again, with hardly any variations. It goes like this: Canadian entrepreneur develops hot idea, sets up company, gets successful in a small way, needs money to expand, goes to banks, goes to government agencies, goes to venture-capital firms, knocks on half the doors in the Toronto-Dominion Centre, gets nowhere; his proposal is met with incomprehension or, at the very best, a cautious display of interest that's followed, weeks later, by a short letter saying no thanks. Entrepreneur, now desperate, meets somebody who knows somebody in New York; introductions are arranged; entrepreneur hops down on the breakfast flight, is greeted in Wall Street office by team of immensely well-informed, immensely receptive American investment bankers. They understand his problems, they've done their homework, they ask the right questions, they do deals like this every day. That same week, sometimes even that same day, he's got his money. No waffling, no referrals to the investment committee that only meets on the third Tuesday of every second month; they make a decision fast and stick to it. Entrepreneur flies back to Toronto that night with the deal in his pocket. He may have signed away most of his company, but he's got the money.

I have heard this scenario so often that I've invented a name for it: the Clamjuice Cocktail Scenario. You see, they used to make an excellent clamjuice cocktail at the members' dining room of the New York Stock Exchange. Fresh tomato juice, tangy essence of Atlantic clams, spiked with just the right amount of gin or vodka. A lot of Canadians have won swift financial reprieves over clamjuice cocktails at places like the NYSE members' dining room; and in the process, a number of potentially important Canadian companies have been consigned to foreign control. To a man, the entrepreneurs who participate in the Clamjuice Cocktail Scenario feel vaguely unhappy about it. Of course they wanted to keep their company Canadian. But when the money people in Toronto or Montreal or Vancouver won't listen to you, what can you do? You hop down to what is still the largest, most sophisticated capital market in the world, and surprisingly often you come back with the money. Better to have 49 percent of something, they reason, than to be left with 100 percent of nothing.

Jeff Bennett is one Canadian who's played out this scenario. He is a vice-president of Consolidated Computer Inc., a firm that had developed the only Canadian computer product that's sold all over the world. It's called a Key-Edit system — basically, a mini-computer that corrects data before it's fed into the big computer. Consolidated was one of those companies that was *too* successful. Computer equipment is leased rather than sold; which meant that every time Consolidated leased one of its hot little Key-Edit units, it had to raise $50,000. The cash-flow shortages were grisly; at one point, the manager of the plant in Ottawa was paying for the office toilet paper out of his own pocket. Eventually, these cash shortages forced Consolidated into receivership, and it took years to claw its way back to solvency.

Anyhow, the Consolidated experience provides as good an example as any of the Clamjuice Cocktail Scenario in action. At one point in the company's fortunes, a federal government agency had agreed with the company to guarantee 90 percent of a $1.5-million bank loan. Bennett and Consolidated's president, Mers Kutt, approached three Canadian banks. Their collateral was the Government of Canada, for God's sake, but all three banks turned them down. "They told us they didn't know the computer industry," says Bennett, "and they felt that if they loaned us the money, it would only be the first of many more requirements, which was true."

And so, as dutiful actors in the Clamjuice script, Kutt and Bennett caught the breakfast flight to New York one morning, and walked in cold to a meeting at the First National City Bank of New York. Bennett recalls the scene: "It's nine o'clock in the morning, okay? I thought we were going to have to make the usual educational pitch, the way you have to do with the Canadian banks — you know, explain the basics, all that. So we go in there, and one guy introduces himself as Joe Doakes who's in charge of the bank's computer section — *in charge* of the computer section, okay? And there are five other guys in the room, and I'm introduced around. This is Joe Smith, he's in charge of data entry products for our computer division. And here's so-and-so, who's interested in peripheral areas. All specialists. *Five* of them!

"So the head guy pulls out this file and says, 'Okay. Consolidated Computer. Here's what we have on you.' And, my God, they have this 30-page updated report on our company, where we stood in the industry, the strides we were making in the U.S., where our marketing offices were, how our product compared to the competition's. It was fantastic.

"Then they got into the questions. No Mickey Mouse stuff. Real questions. Why do you use a fixed-head storage device when your competitor uses a moving-head device? What's the memory cycle time? And then they got into other areas — our marketing strategy, our pricing strategy, how the product works — I mean, they knew our company. Not because they'd been expecting us to ask them for a loan, but because they'd made it their business to know the industry.

"It was one of the toughest financial meetings I've ever had, and one of the most enjoyable. Geez, here were financial men who actually knew what they were talking about! As bankers, they took the attitude that, hey, we hope you need *lots* of money. They wanted to lend it to us, because that was their business. I can't describe how good I felt after that meeting."

By the end of the week, Consolidated had offers from not one, but two New York banks. It signed with one. For the next year, the other bank kept in touch by long-distance telephone; if you ever need anything, was the message, we're here to help.

Entrepreneurs spend most of their time trying to persuade

people to give them money, either as a loan or as an investment in the company's shares. This search for money has an obsessional quality about it, like a heavy drug habit. The more cash you shoot into the corporate veins, the more you seem to need. As the company progresses from the initial gleam in the eye, through the development phase, the prototype phase, the production phase, the expansion phase, the search for cash grows more consuming, since larger and larger sums are almost always required. By this time, the entrepreneur feels a heavy emotional obligation — not only to the idea that has consumed his life for years, but to the people who have shared his faith by working for, and investing in, the company. He knows that everything he's worked for, everything his associates have worked for, is riding on his ability to persuade someone to put up more cash. Nearly always, that someone is a man who is paid to listen all day to similar pitches, and who nearly always says no — a banker, a bureaucrat in some government agency, a venture capitalist, a stockbroker who underwrites issues of new companies.

A substantial mythology has grown up around this process of raising capital, most of it centred on the legendary unwillingness of Canadian financial institutions to risk their money. The banks: "They won't lend you money unless you can convince them you don't need it." The venture-capital outfits: "Those bastards —they all play squash together at the Cambridge Club. If you get turned down by one, you've been turned down by all of them." The investment houses: "All they wanted for selling my stock was an arm and a leg." Government agencies, such as the Industrial Development Bank: "Jesus — try to get an answer out of them! Red tape like you wouldn't believe. Lord spare me from the bureaucrats."

Those are actual quotes from actual businessmen, and beneath them all you can detect the whine of the rejected suitor. From those who did the rejecting, however, you get a different story. The stock market wasn't ripe; they wanted too much money, or too little; the company didn't have a "track record" — that is, a history of solid profitability; there wasn't enough management depth. If you spend time, as I have, talking to entrepreneurs who are chasing money, and to people who are in the business of providing that money to young companies, you soon discover that you're dealing with different kinds of people. It's almost as though there were two cultures, the entrepreneurial culture and the investment culture, each of them with radically different views of the world. The founders of companies are usually men possessed by a vision. And they find it hard to relate to the bankers, the venture capitalists, the money men who examine hundreds of such visions every year, and judge most of them wanting. That's why the Clamjuice Cocktail Scenario, as it's been experienced by scores of Canadian risk takers, seems to express so much about the shortcomings of Canadian capital markets. Entrepreneurs like Jeff Bennett of Consolidated Computer, when they make the pilgrimage to Wall Street, feel as though they've come home. After months of fund-grubbing in a northern climate that seems prim and anal and hostile to all forms of risk, they suddenly discover a capitalist Shangri-la where financial people, men who control institutions that control other people's money, think exactly as they do.

This disparity is often ascribed to psychological differences between Canadians and Americans. Canadians, according to this theory, are prudent, unventuresome, uninventive; Americans are innovators, plungers, gamblers, risk takers. We're cautious; they're not. The differences in approach are real enough. But I think it's simplistic to ascribe them to "national character." If Canadians "don't invent things," if Canadians "don't take risks," it's not because of some mysterious defect in our collective psyche. Instead, it's the result of an historical process which has left us with a strong tradition of *public* entrepreneurship (by no means a bad thing), and an excessively weak tradition of private risk taking — unless it's imported risk taking.

In fact, Canadians do invent things. As J. J. Brown has demonstrated in his authoritative study of Canadian innovation, *Ideas in Exile*, "Canadians have made contributions to world science and technology out of all proportion to their small number." Even before the age of steam, a Yarmouth, N.S., inventor named John Patch, who eventually ended up in the poorhouse, in 1833 built and demonstrated what may have been the world's first screw propeller. The first rotary snowplow, for blowing snow off railroad tracks, was patented by a Toronto dentist named J. W. Elliott in 1869. Bell's invention of the telephone in Brantford was only the best-known of an astonishing record of Canadian innovation: half-tone plates for reproducing photographs in newspapers (George Desbarats, Montreal, circa 1870); the photographic developing tank (Arthur McCurdy, 1899); the panoramic camera (John Connon, Elora, Ontario, 1887); the first commercially practical electron microscope (University of Toronto, 1938); wirephoto (William Stephenson, 1923). Edward S. Rogers of Toronto invented — and later manufactured — the first radios that could operate on house current instead of batteries. Canadian National engineers in Montreal built the world's first diesel electric locomotive in 1929. Morse Robb, of Belleville, Ontario, invented the electronic organ in 1927. "If Canadians had taken advantage of their opportunity to become the world's supplier of electronic organs, the way the Swiss have become world suppliers of watches," writes Brown, "that one item alone would have been enough each year to reverse our international trade position and give us a favorable balance."

Brown's book makes depressing reading, for it is a century-long litany of missed opportunities. Every time a Canadian invented something, the Canadian financial community declined to back it, and some foreigner did. There are literally dozens of Canadian inventions, Brown demonstrates, which could, if properly exploited, have grown into major Canadian industries. "By and large," he concludes, "we are a timid people, afraid of ourselves and terrified by the demands of the real world. In every area of human activity — art, business, literature, education — we have been content to let others take the risk of presenting new ideas to a fiercely resisting world . . . This is our basic problem as a nation: a conservatism carried to the extreme of idiocy. If not corrected soon, it will leave us unable to compete as an industrial nation in the modern world."

But is it really some psychic defect that's to blame, some failure of the collective nerve? Or is the defect *structural* — a failure of institutions? How is our collective risk-taking capacity affected, for instance, by the fact that there are only a handful of consequential banks in the whole country — whereas, in the U.S. there are literally thousands? Is it purely a consequence of national character that Canadian insurance companies, sitting as they do upon billions and billions of dollars worth of almost involuntary savings, have invested a far smaller proportion of those funds in the stock of young Canadian companies than they're allowed to do? Was it national character that prompted one bank to refuse a loan to an employee group that was trying to buy their own company, and then turned around and loaned the money to a U.S. firm that wanted to take it over? Or was it simply the consequences of an outmoded set of institutional arrangements?

There are very precise restrictions, spelled out in the Bank Act and in the acts regulating insurance, loan and trust companies, specifying the kinds of investments that such companies may make. The Canadian and British Insurance Companies Act, for instance, prohibits insurance companies, except in rare circumstances, from making loans that aren't fully secured, unless the borrowing company has a long record of financial stability. Under the same Act, the insurance companies are also prohibited from buying shares in a company unless that company has an unbroken five-year record of paying or being able to pay dividends. In any event, they're not allowed to own more than the 30 percent of the shares of any corporation, unless such investments are directly related to the insurance business. There is, however, a "basket clause" in the Insurance Act which allows insurance companies to invest up to seven percent of their assets in somewhat riskier situations.

Similar restrictions apply to trust and loan companies, to pension funds, and to banks. Under the Bank Act, for instance, banks aren't normally allowed to own more than 10 percent of any Canadian corporation. An exception arises when the bank's investment is less than $5 million. In that case, providing the company is *not* a loan or trust company, the bank may own up to 50 percent of the voting stock. The overall regulatory pattern is clear. The law quite properly prohibits financial institutions from taking immoderate risks with other people's savings.

Many financial institutions have put money into venture-capital firms, thus permitting arm's-length participation in the financing of young companies. But none of them has made enough venture-capital investments, either through venture-capital firms or directly, to come anywhere near the ceilings the law allows. The bank that's come closest is the Toronto-Dominion. In a survey of capital sources, Russell M. Knight of the University of Western Ontario found that the TD was the only bank to make venture-capital investments directly. The TD also attempted to set up its own venture-capital subsidiary called the TD Capital Group, but the regulatory authorities vetoed the proposal.

In the overwhelming number of cases, however, the law is no barrier. Our major financial institutions don't support young firms mostly because (a) they don't know how to evaluate them — that's why they sometimes invest in venture-capital firms that do — and because (b) they can get better returns elsewhere. Why take risks with untried young companies when you can get high, painless returns from lending instruments like mortgages, or even Chargex cards?

And so young Canadian companies starve for funds, while billions of dollars of Canadian savings are invested elsewhere. Even a minor change in institutional policies would improve the situation, but no such change is forthcoming. The pension funds, Professor Knight wrote, "now hold such a large portfolio that even a small fraction of one percent of their funds directed into venture capital would overwhelm the total amount of capital available for venture capital situations currently." Water, water everywhere, but not a drop to drink.

It would take a separate book to explore all the shortcomings in our capital markets, and ways of overcoming them. But it's at least possible to demonstrate that Canadians — as distinct from the institutions that deploy their savings — are no more "cautious" than Americans. By 1968, for instance, Canadians had more than $32 billion worth of savings socked into insurance, pension and mutual funds, plus another $15 billion invested directly in the stock market. Indeed, there is some evidence to suggest that Canadians, in relative terms, are even more dedicated investors than Americans. Professor G. R. Conway of York University, by analyzing 1968 taxation statistics, discovered that dividend income — that is, income from common stock investments — was a relatively more important source of investment income for Canadians than it was for Americans, in all but the lowest income groups. Conway also concluded, in the same study, for the Toronto Stock Exchange, that there was no shortage of development capital in Canada. If anything, in fact, there was a shortage of suitable Canadian investment vehicles to absorb all those billions of dollars of spare cash.

The equation, in other words, seems to consist of billions of dollars seeking a home on the one hand and hundreds of struggling young firms seeking cash on the other. Why don't they connect? As the Gray Report on foreign investment rather mildly expressed it: "For one reason or another the process of bringing borrower and lender together is not carried out satisfactorily. This in itself is evidence of a weakness in the allocative function of the markets." Canada's large financial institutions, which are well equipped to meet the capital needs of big business, haven't yet learned to serve the firms that hope to become the big businesses of tomorrow.

That's the gap on one side of the equation. On the other side, there are equally apparent shortcomings in the expertise and sophistication of Canadian entrepreneurs. Bankers, venture capitalists, officials in government lending agencies are almost unanimous on this point. They examine hundreds of worthwhile proposals every year, ideas with genuine potential. But they judge that the men proposing them lack the experience and financial sophistication to carry them forward. Professor Knight of Western cited this problem in his 1973 survey of venture-capital firms in Canada. It's an axiom in the venture-capital business that you don't invest in ideas; you invest in people. And many of the people whom the venture-capital firms evaluate don't have the foggiest notion of how to run a business. "The main problem raised by all venture capitalists," writes Professor Knight, "was that there is definitely a lack of capable venture management in the companies which brought proposals to them . . . This was also the attitude of American companies responding to the question of whether there was any significant difference between American ventures they normally assessed and any Canadian ventures they may have seen in the past. They replied that there seemed to be a significant difference in the management ability present in the venture proposals they received, with Canadian management lagging behind that in the U.S."

Professors Litvak and Maule of Carleton found the same shortcomings when they surveyed 47 small high-technology firms and the men who ran them: "Most of the entrepreneurs were ill-prepared to organize and manage a newly established venture. Their level of competence in such management areas as marketing, finance, personnel and even manufacturing was sadly lacking.

"Technological entrepreneurs," Maule and Litvak wrote, "may find themselves so preoccupied with raising capital, generating marketing opportunities and performing other administrative duties, that they are unable to devote the required effort to managing the commercialization of the innovation. Unwillingness to delegate control even in the technical area or an inability to impart the technical know-how to one's subordinates, often led to unnecessary complications and delays which had the effect of undermining the total operation. Further, the very drive and enthusiasm which led to the formation of the enterprise, namely, the entrepreneur's technical innovative skills, became partially dissipated when he expanded his activities into areas in which he had limited competence."

But enough of shortcomings. It's difficult to raise money for new ventures; but then, it nearly always has been. This may even be part of the fitness of things. For there have been times in recent history when money was readily available for new ventures; when a mere promise of novelty was sufficient to attract millions of eager, unheeding dollars. The mid-1960s was such a time. So was the mid-1920s. Both were unhealthy investment climates, in which innovation was used to fuel speculation, with the inevitable aftermath.

Now we inhabit a grimmer, less romantic time, but the realities of raising money are the same as they always were. If you're an entrepreneur, you must try to get it (a) from your friends and relatives; or (b) from your bank manager; or (c) by "going public" —selling shares in your company or; (d) by approaching one of several dozen Canadian venture-capital firms, which are in the business of investing in young companies; or (e) by applying for a loan or grant from some provincial or federal agency that's been set up to assist small business.

Different sources of financing tend to apply at different stages in a company's development. The personal savings of friends, relatives and the entrepreneur himself are obviously the most readily available sources at the very earliest, gleam-in-the-eye stages. But they can only carry a company so far. Bank loans, which are short-term almost by definition, are common and appropriate in the sort of small businesses where the initial investment is low, and the anticipated returns will be fairly immediate: a shoe store, say. But most banks simply aren't interested in longer time spans, or in the large risks involved in financing young manufacturing companies. The stock-market route is similarly unpromising. Until a company has reached a respectable size, and is generating substantial revenues, it usually isn't feasible to float a public stock issue. William P. Wilder, then president of Wood Gundy Securities Ltd., once told Clive Baxter of The Financial Post the main reason for turning down companies that wanted to go public: "They don't need enough money. They're talking about $100,000 to $300,000, and you can't really do a public issue for that amount. There's just not a good enough aftermarket for the shares."

Wilder's comment points up one of the most glaring weaknesses of the "allocative function of the markets" that the Gray Report mentioned: the inability to deliver financing to firms in the earlier stages of their development. The classic bind, especially in innovative technological companies, is when the entrepreneur raises enough money to begin development of a new product, then fails to raise the funds necessary to complete the job. It's no great trick to set up a company and plug along for a year or two on product development; and once the product is established in the market and generating profits, the chances of securing bank financing or a public stock issue aren't wholly remote. It's in the middle range, in the stage of corporate adolescence, where the great gap exists.

In the late 1960s, a new kind of financial institution emerged in Canada to fill it: the venture-capital firm. The idea behind them is as old as capitalism. Much of Britain's colonial expansion, and the early development of the U.S., was funded by private merchant banks which took large financial risks in young ventures, in the expectation of large rewards later on. Canada never developed a merchant banking tradition of its own, but the venture firms are now doing their best to develop one. There are about 50 firms in Canada, most of them based in Toronto, that specialize full-time in providing "seed money" to promising young companies. Most of them consist of no more than half a dozen bright young men who spend their days evaluating the proposals of people who come before them seeking financial backing. The whole idea, as one firm's brochure expresses it, is "not to invest in blue chips, but to assist in the creation of the blue chips of tomorrow." The theory is that if you can find the right man with the right idea, and if you back him early enough, and if you're prepared to nursemaid the venture for as long as seven to 10 years — which appears to be the normal gestation period for a technologically based Canadian manufacturing company — you might wind up making a large profit.

Venture capitalists, not only make loans; they also buy shares in young companies. The per-share price is usually a few dollars, or even a few pennies, and the initial investment is usually in the $200,000-$500,000 range. If the company prospers, those shares could be worth hundreds of times what the venture firm paid for them; and it is this expectation of immoderate profits that justifies the immoderate risks.

American Research and Development Corp., a Boston-based firm founded in 1946, is considered the granddaddy of the industry, and some of· ARDC's early gambles (such as Teledyne and Digital Equipment) are legends in the trade. In 25 years of backing young companies, ARDC invested $23.6 million in the stock of young companies that later became worth more than $300 million.

Coups like this, although extremely rare, have tended to infuse the venture capital business with an aura of glamour. The day-to-day reality, however, is fairly mundane. The venture firm's management team might be approached with several hundred proposals a year. Most can be dismissed on the basis of a five-minute phone call; other evaluations may take weeks of an executive's time. For most venture firms, it's a very big year if they end up investing in more than half a dozen projects.

The forms of investment vary. Some venture firms make loans, others buy shares, others choose a mixture of debt and equity. They seldom buy majority controls; in return for their investment, they usually acquire between 20 and 30 percent of the company. In return, the entrepreneur must sacrifice varying degrees of his independence. Nearly all venture firms insist on placing a representative on the company's board of directors, and demand a veto over major corporate decisions, which may include matters of salaries, dividends, external investments and big expenditures. Some venture firms have even been known to insist on countersigning the company's cheques. Venture firms hardly ever play the silent-partner role; most expect to take an active part in shaping policy of the companies they invest in. Some even charge for this service, like management consultants.

The most successful investment, from the venture firm's point of view, is the one that requires the least monitoring, the least hand-holding, the least expenditure of executive time. Once the investment is made, it quickly becomes apparent whether it's a success or a failure. Most such investments, however, become what venture capitalists call "the living dead" — companies that neither fail nor succeed spectacularly, but require endless time-consuming attention.

Where does the venture money come from? Some is family money, but many venture firms are financed by banks, insurance companies and other financial institutions. The government-owned Canada Development Corp. now owns a piece of three venture firms, and has thus subcontracted the task of evaluating potential investments. What all venture firms are looking for is that rare company with quite fantastic growth prospects, usually the product of a brilliant idea combined with brilliant management. They have to feel very enthusiastic about a company's prospects, in other words, before they'll invest at all. Professor Knight, in his survey of Canadian venture firms, asked them what kind of return they expected on their investments. Some expected the value to triple in five years; others expected their investment to quintuple in two years; one firm expected a 2,400 percent return within four years; the most conservative expectation he found was a growth rate of 10 percent per year. These aren't hopes. They're *criteria* — if the venture firms can't hope for fat profits in a relatively short time, they don't want to invest at all.

What they expect and what they get, of course, are two different things. The venture-capital business is still too new in Canada to make accurate estimates of how well it has performed. But many of them were founded in the late 1960s, as a by-product of a stock-market euphoria that turned out to be transitory, and none of them has done nearly as well as the granddaddy of the industry, the legend-making American Research and Development Corp.

Part of the problem may be that most venture firms aren't sufficiently venturesome. Despite the industry's go-go reputation, many venture firms are as cautious as banks (that, after all, is often the source of their capital), and just as insistent on a "track record." Professor Knight's survey found that fewer than one third of the investments made by the 50 firms he studied were in firms at the concept, start-up or development stage. "In general," he concluded, "the early years of a company, before a track record was established and before market penetration could be achieved, were by far the most difficult in which to obtain funds. This result tends to confirm . . . that venture capital in Canada is available primarily for expansion of established companies rather than for start-up or initial operation. The fact that the user company does not have a history of profitable operation usually prevents it from obtaining funds, not only from the banks but from venture-capital companies as well."

Which leaves various forms of government support, such as the federally sponsored Industrial Development Bank, provincial agencies such as the Ontario Development Corp., and the myriad of aid-to-business programs offered by the federal Department of Industry, Trade and Commerce. Here again, the emphasis is on financing or assisting established companies. Indeed, I've heard entrepreneurs complain that some government funding agencies, which are supposed to supplement the functions of chartered banks, are more cautious than the banks themselves.

The IDB was designed as a small-business bank. It has bought shares in companies on only two or three occasions, and all its loans are fully secured. Still, it's usually the first place that entrepreneurs look when they're seeking money; it lends more money each year than all other federal and provincial lending institutions combined.

About half its loans are for $25,000 or less, and about half of these are advanced for the purchase of land or buildings. And the IDB tends to concentrate on service businesses — laundries, pool halls, restaurants, wholesale and retail trade. The proportion of its loans to manufacturing businesses has been steadily declining — from 29 percent in 1968 to around 22 percent in 1972. And because British Columbia, until recently, was without a provincial lending institution, the IDB lent more money in that province than anywhere else. Elsewhere in the country, small-business loans from the chartered banks, through subsidiaries such as Roy-Nat, have tended to take up the slack. This pattern has prompted criticism that the IDB, instead of acting as a lender of last resort, is too often competing on the same terms with private lending institutions. There's no question that the IDB has played a useful role in financing small business. But, like the chartered banks which it is sometimes accused of competing against, its role is far too limited in the start-up and development stages of young manufacturing companies.

One of the more promising sources of support for innovative, high-technology companies are the various incentive and assistance programs of the federal Department of Industry, Trade and Commerce. ITC officials stress that they're not in the venture-capital business. Nevertheless, some of their programs offer incentives that make it easier to finance new-product development. The best-known is the assistance offered under the Industrial Research and Development Incentives Act (know by its acronym, IRDIA). Under IRDIA, the government makes grants to companies doing business in Canada that undertake scientific research and development, so long as it's deemed to be "of benefit to Canada." The grants usually amount to about 25 percent of what the company spent on capital expenditures required for an R & D program, plus 25 percent of the company's current expenditures over and above its usual R & D budget. These grants are tax-free, and some companies choose to take them in the form of income tax credits. Whatever form of payment is chosen, the grants are "retrospective." The company must go ahead and spend its own R & D money, in other words, then submit its figures to ITC at the end of the year. Most companies, however, check in advance with ITC officials, who will give advance opinions on which parts of a proposed R & D program are likely to qualify for grants after the money has been spent.

Another ITC incentive program that is of major benefit to high-technology companies is the Program for the Advancement of Industrial Technology (PAIT), which provides "financial assistance for selected projects concerned with the development of new or improved products and processes which incorporate new technology and offer good prospects for commercial exploitation in domestic and international markets." PAIT grants cover up to half the estimated costs of a development project, and these can include the costs of market research as well as straight development costs.

ITC also administers the Industrial Design Assistance Program (IDAP), which makes grants of up to half the cost of designing a new product — designers' salaries, plus administrative and operational expenses, plus consultants' fees in some cases.

ITC also administers an acronymic blizzard of programs aimed at assisting specific industries, or companies in specific situations. The Program to Enhance Productivity (PEP) pays up to half the cost, up to $50,000, of efficiency studies aimed at improving productivity. GAAP (General Adjustment Assistance Program) guarantees private loans and makes loans and grants to firms whose products are fighting foreign competition. DIP (Defense Industry Productivity Program) assists firms that want to compete for defense contracts. PIDA (Pharmaceutical Industry Development Assistance) helps drug firms upgrade efficiency.

Most of the companies profiled in this book have availed themselves of assistance under one or more of ITC's programs. Performance Sailcraft Inc. received a grant when Ian Bruce was developing the Laser sailboat. Trident Aircraft Ltd. couldn't have got its plane into the air without assistance under PAIT and IR-DIA. Bombardier has received federal assistance under various programs. So have Cox Systems and Benson Industries and ATCO Industries. For any Canadian company that's trying to develop something new, federal assistance is a fact of life, and often an important factor in its survival.

It should be stressed that federal officials, like bankers or venture capitalists or any other capital source, are in the business of deploying other people's money — in this case, the taxpayer's; and they're no more prone to gamble it on untried ventures than any other institution. They demand to see a "track record"; not as a guarantee of future profitability so much as an assurance that the company has the resources and experience to carry out what it says it needs federal assistance to attempt. This means that all applications are investigated carefully, even creatively. If a company's application fails to qualify for one program, ITC officials

34

have been known to steer the company to another program where it will qualify. And, although they're not venture capitalists, the ITC officials who evaluate the applications are fully conversant with the industry involved; most of them used to work in the private sector themselves.

Yes, there are complaints of red tape, bureaucratic labyrinths, unexplained delays, shortness of vision. But most of them come from companies whose applications have been rejected. With a few exceptions, the entrepreneurs in this book whose companies have been recipients of federal assistance spoke highly of the relationship. Since a single ITC official usually deals with a project from application to completion, the working relationships that develop aren't characterized by the hostility and mutual incomprehension that you find in most transactions between business and government. Indeed, a sense of partnership sometimes develops between the entrepreneur and the government man; he fights for the project within his own department, he worries about its prospects, he becomes as committed to the project as the man who initiated it.

Most of the money, however, goes to fairly large companies, a disconcertingly large number of which are foreign-controlled. In Canada, when you say big companies, you usually mean U.S.-controlled companies; which means that a little less than half the money handed out by ITC as incentive grants goes to foreign-controlled firms. Between 1965 and 1970, the Grey Report discovered, ITC distributed nearly $21 million in incentives under PAIT alone; $9.7 million of that money went to foreign-controlled firms. Nearly $45 million was paid out under IRDIA during the same period, and at least $19 million of it went to foreign-controlled firms. The proportion was even higher for grants made under various defense industry incentive programs. Under DIP, for instance, Canadian firms were paid $3,528,000; non-resident firms, in the same period, benefitted by more than $26 million.

That sum represents one of many odd anomalies in the way capital is deployed in the country. At a time when dozens of genuinely deserving Canadian companies were struggling to get off the ground, Canadian taxpayers spent $26 million assisting foreign-controlled companies to profit from foreign defense contracts. But that's the kind of anomaly you're going to get in an economy so heavily dominated by foreign investment. The thing feeds on itself. The more foreign capital we accept, the more accommodating to further incursions our financial institutions become.

I didn't intend this to become yet another sermon on economic nationalism. But really, that's what this whole book is about. Our approach to entrepreneurship determines to a large extent what kind of a country our children will inherit, if there's anything left to inherit. Either we encourage our own entrepreneurs, or we continue to invite them in from outside to do the job for us. And if we continue doing that, our potential as a manufacturing nation will never be realized.

Canadians have grown prosperous on a resource-based economy. But it's becoming increasingly apparent that that kind of prosperity can't continue indefinitely. As Walter Gordon has observed, the situation is analogous to that of a farmer who doesn't grow anything, but maintains his lifestyle by selling off a piece of his property each year. We must become a manufacturing country, in other words, or we won't be a country at all.

3

HOW DAVE HAZLEWOOD
TOOK A DREAM
AND MADE IT FLY

For me, there was a particular moment when the Trigull 320, the first light aircraft to be developed in Canada in almost a decade, stopped being a cunning assemblage of wires and struts and aluminum sheeting and became a machine that might actually fly. It happened on August 3, 1973, two days before the first test flight. The Trigull had looked like an airplane for weeks. The engine was mounted up behind the cockpit. The instruments were installed on the control panel and above it. The red and brown speed lines had been painted on the white fuselage a few days before. If you pressed a certain button on the control panel, you heard an electric whine, and the wing flaps actually moved up and down. The thing had all the parts a plane is supposed to have, but to me it still didn't feel like an airplane.

I'd been hanging out in Trident's factory — maybe workshop is a better word — for more than a week, watching mechanics fiddle with wires, listening to the almost incomprehensible jargon of aeronautical engineers, watching metal parts being shaped by tools I didn't understand. Day after day, the Trigull stood on the factory floor, while men in white coveralls crawled all over it. I'd seen aluminum panels removed to reveal what looked like small clothesline pulleys — part of the control systems that would actually steer the plane. I'd seen the engineers spend several days putting together a fibreglass baffle that would fit over the motor and steer currents of air inside the cowling, so that each of the engine's six cylinders would cool properly. They faced an infinity of tinkerers' small problems: adjusting wires and pulleys so that a flap would lower 30 degrees, instead of 32; designing an extra piece of aluminum to brace the tail so it wouldn't wobble in flight; replacing the sleek windshield for better visibility. I'd seen the thing coming together, in other words, as a collection of discrete parts. And even now, two days before the first flight, with the plane parked outside a hangar at Vancouver International Airport, as test pilot Paul Hartman prepared to start the motor, the plane was still only an object, a collection of mechanical problems and solutions, a clean piece of sculpture, but still a thing merely, with no life of its own.

The preparations for a test flight never go smoothly. The whole point of the exercise is to isolate and solve technical problems on the ground, so they won't become disasters in the air. But now, after nearly a week of last-minute tinkering, the Trigull was ready to move under its own power for the first time. The engine had been started several times in the past few days, and had been given 100 hours of bench testing before that. But this time the engine refused to start. Hartman, a bandy-legged man in his 50s who's flown everything from Sopwith Camels to CF-100s, kept running the starter. The propeller turned slowly on the battery, and gasoline — the overflow from Hartman's priming of the motor — dribbled through a special outlet and onto the runway. Chuck Herbst, the American engineer who'd been designing this plane in his head for the past eight years, stood with his hand resting on the end of one wing, watching Hartman in the cockpit. "Jesus," Herbst muttered, to no one in particular. The starting motor continued to whine, the propeller slowly revolved. A mechanic was up on the wing, kneeling down, peering at the lifeless engine, the palm of his hand suspended above one cylinder, coaxing. You could see wavy gasoline vapors wafting from the exhaust.

Then somebody shouted "Fire!" and everybody was running at once. In much less than a second, a belch of orange flame spouted out from the exhaust; someone ran forward toward the cockpit, yelling "Fire!" at Hartman; someone else raced up with a fire extinguisher. But, before he got near the plane, the engine mysteriously started with a lovely, deep-throated roar and instantly snuffed out the flame that threatened to set back by several months the development of the Canadian light aircraft industry.

Hartman, the test pilot, listened as Herbst, the designer, shouted a few last-minute words through the open cockpit door. Then he slammed it shut, gunned the engine, and the Trigull began to move.

Dave Hazlewood, the crewcut engineer and amateur pilot who is president of Trident Aircraft Ltd., the young Vancouver-based company that is developing the Trigull, frowned as the plane turned on the tarmac. The nose wheel, one of the trickiest design jobs in the whole aircraft, was flopping sideways at an odd angle, like the wheel on a supermarket cart when the socket is loose. "Those wheel springs aren't strong enough," he said to Herbst. "It flops from one side to the other."

I still couldn't believe I was seeing an airplane. Hartman taxied it about 100 feet, then paused, the engine running smoothly now and sounding lovely. Mechanics placed wooden blocks in front of all three wheels as Hartman prepared for an engine power test. He reached up and pushed the throttle, and the noise began to mount. The Trigull was powered by a 320-horsepower Teledyne-Continental Tiara 6 320, a U.S.-built engine which, at this point, hadn't yet been certified by the U.S. Federal Aviation Administration. Most aircraft engines sound harsh and blatty, but the noise that the Tiara 6 320 made was a sort of mighty, amplified purr.

And that was the moment, just as Hartman revved up the engine to full acceleration, when that pretty little airplane transformed itself before my eyes. You could see the plane straining forward against its restraints. The fuselage almost seemed to stretch visibly, and I had this sudden flash of wonder: *My God — it's alive! She wants to fly!* If Hartman had released the brakes, the Trigull would have rocketed down the runway and, yes, up into the air. But that would come later. Hartman, satisfied with the engine test, cut the motor and stepped out, grinning. "She taxis like a Cadillac," he told Hazlewood.

That was when I noticed a strange thing. For as long as I'd been hanging around the Trigull, the builders referred to the machine as "it." But from then on, after that first miracle of motion across 100 feet of tarmac, the plane suddenly acquired feminine gender. Everybody called the Trigull "she." She'd come to life, acquired a personality, become herself. An airplane had been born before my eyes.

The way to get a fishy stare from Dave Hazlewood is to suggest, as several newspapers have done, that the Trigull 320 is "the successor to the Seabee." True, they're both light amphibious aircraft. True, they share a strong family resemblance, with a pusher propeller mounted above the wing and behind the cockpit, and — at least in the prototype Trigull — with the same bottle-shaped nose. There's even a family connection between the designers. Percival Spencer, the man who designed the Seabee for Republic Aviation in the late 1940s, is the father-in-law of Chuck Herbst. Both Hazlewood and his partner, Paddy Newton, who founded Trident Aircraft Ltd. in 1969 to finish the job that Herbst had begun four years earlier, had been Seabee owners for years, and loved their planes in the exasperated way that a father loves a slightly slow-witted son. "But the Trigull isn't a successor to anything," says Hazlewood. "The plane was designed from the ground up. If you're going to build a light amphibian, there are only a few configurations you can use. The one we chose happened to be the same as the Seabee's."

So, despite all the similarities, the Trigull isn't the successor to anything. Rather, it's a fresh attempt, utilizing all the new technology that's been developed over the last 25 years, to build a light but roomy single-engined amphibious aircraft. "The Trigull," says Newton, "is what the Seabee would have become if it stayed in production. But nothing is interchangeable with the Seabee."

Republic Aviation built 1,050 Seabees in 1946 and 1947, thereby creating one of aviation's more lovable eccentrics. For one thing, it combined a roomy cockpit with an engine that wasn't very powerful. This meant, as more than one Seabee pilot has abruptly discovered, that the plane was temptingly easy to overload. When overloaded, it had an awkward tendency to fly into mountains, since it couldn't fly above them.

The Seabee had other shortcomings. It was slow — cruising speed was 103 miles per hour; the water rudder is generally considered to be as useless as the heater on an early Volkswagen; the main landing gear is too narrow, which makes it tricky to taxi in a crosswind; and, until the wings were lengthened in later modifications, the wingspan was too short to deliver adequate lift.

But most people who have flown it consider the Seabee a wonderful aircraft. "I owned my second Seabee for nine years," says Paddy Newton, "and it gave me absolutely no trouble whatsoever. It never missed a beat, never failed to start — even though I'd leave it idle for as long as two or three months at a time. Honestly, that plane was the very finest. Hell, why would I, a fellow who can afford a brand-new Cessna, fly an old Seabee? And why do Seabees that sold for maybe $3,000 in the 1950s fetch something like $10,000 today? Let's face it — it was the strongest and most versatile aircraft available for coastal operations."

A few of those 1,050 Seabees are plastered against various mountains along the Pacific coast. But hundreds are still in operation, either as commercial workhorses or owned by private pilots who tinker with them, dream about them, cherish them, and form clubs to exchange Seabee lore — and, more cogently, Seabee parts — with other of the brethren. That's how Paddy Newton, an ex-RAF type who bought his first Seabee in 1950, met Dave Hazlewood, who owned five Seabees before deciding to build his own version. Both were members of the Vancouver Seabee Club, and both were passionately attached to this machine that had enriched both their lives and, on at least two occasions, almost ended them.

Hazlewood's near miss happened in 1963, shortly after he'd taken off from Sproat Lake on Vancouver Island, with a full complement of passengers, plus a full load of baggage. As soon as he was airborne and heading for the trees that rim the lake, Hazlewood discovered that the plane refused to climb. Somehow, with a lot of praying and a lot of nerve, he made it to the next landing. "But it was an *interesting* experience," he says. "I was able to see the top of each individual tree as we went by. Treetops have held quite a fascination for me ever since."

Newton had his own near miss in 1955, during a takeoff from Butedale, a small upcoast fishing settlement. Halfway into his climb, the Seabee's engine quit. Newton made a terrifying forced landing, downwind. The water was so rough that, as the plane skimmed the water, a wave smashed over the cockpit. For one shuddering instant, Newton thought his plane must have plowed straight into the chuck. But then the waters magically receded, daylight reappeared, and Newton realized he was in no worse shape than, say, a dinghy in a North Atlantic squall. He calmly pulled out an oar, paddled across a mile of choppy water back to Butedale, fixed the motor and resumed his journey.

Those are the kind of stories Seabee owners enjoy telling each other, just as scuba divers, when they get together, tend to swap horror stories about sharks. And it was through the Seabee Club that Newton and Hazlewood heard about a California project that was attempting to build a new light amphibian in the Seabee tradition, but which had foundered for lack of funds.

It is a week before the test flight. The Trigull is standing on the factory floor, and several technicians are going over it with what look like large stethoscopes. This exercise is known as flutter testing, which is a way of discovering whether your plane will fly cleanly, or shake to pieces in the air. Every aircraft in flight vibrates like a collection of tuning forks, so you must design it so that all these various jiggles and jounces and flutters of wings, tail-plane, engine mounting and fuselage balance each other out and work smoothly together. If you've designed the plane wrong, the vibration in, say, the rear stabilizer could reinforce sympathetic vibrations in, say, the left wingtip — and shake the damn thing off. When the Trigull was designed, all these intricate mathematical relationships between the vibration modes of various parts of the aircraft were worked out on a computer.

Now some experts from Seattle are methodically jiggling each part of the airplane, using a vibrating device that looks like the paint mixer from a hardware store, and measuring the flutters this motion sets up in other parts of the airplane. They're trying to make sure that all parts of the plane will vibrate in flight the way the computers say they're supposed to.

Using this method, they've already detected one bug today. At a certain vibration frequency, the plane's tail displays an unacceptable amount of motion. Machinists are already at work elsewhere in the factory, building an extra stiffener.

42

Jeff Dean, a young engineer from Seattle, is in charge of the flight flutter tests. He has a sheaf of computer printout spread out on the table in front of him, and he's comparing it to the readings from an oscilloscope, which records the flutters that the technicians are picking up with their stethoscopes. "I got 39.8," he says to the man at the oscilloscope. "You want me to tell you what we predicted? Thirty-nine point nine!" He laughs. "Every once in a while something shakes out right!"

At the end of the day, Dean has coffee with Paul Hartman, who's been paying close attention to the tests. Once, during a test flight of the CF-100, Hartman was diving at 8.7 Gs when he felt a rumble from somewhere in the rear of the airplane. He looked out the cockpit canopy and saw one surface vibrating like a hummingbird's wing. "You could *see* it," Hartman recalls — a good, thick blur maybe 12 inches wide." He pulled out of that dive in a hurry, and ever since he has taken a keen personal interest in flutter tests.

"The airplane shakes out beautifully," Dean was saying as he sipped his coffee. "Everything's real tight. I've shaken airplanes that are so damned sloppy — well, I'm real impressed. Most prototypes are held together with body-filler and five-minute epoxy. Here, the workmanship is phenomenal. You've got a real clean little airplane."

Every entrepreneurial project starts as a gleam in somebody's eye, and the gleam that led to the Trigull first appeared in the eye of a businessman from Everett, Washington, named Bob Dent. Dent owns a company called Tyee Aircraft, which had grown intermittently prosperous as a subcontractor to Boeing. Dent also owned a float-equipped Cessna 180, and used it to commute to a small island he owns in Sproat Lake on Vancouver Island. One weekend, Dent dropped in to a resort lodge on the lake, and ran into a man who shared his interest in amphibious aircraft: none other than Percival Spencer, the man who designed the original three-seater amphibian that became the Republic Seabee. Sitting in front of the big fireplace at Klitsa Lodge, the two men talked of airplanes they'd known, and airplanes they'd like to see. By the end of the evening, they'd decided to become partners in a new venture: to put together a metal home-built amphibian — the kind that could be sold in kits. Later, they approached Spencer's son-in-law, Chuck Herbst, who was then chief project engineer at Aeronca Inc., in Torrance, California, who agreed to become chief engineer. Under U.S. tax regulations, Dent's company, Tyee Aircraft, was able to channel part of its profits into the new project, and still come through a fiscal year with acceptable after-tax earnings. Dent and Spencer anticipated costs of $125,000 to design a prototype that the FAA would certify. After that, Tyee planned to manufacture the parts and sell them to enthusiasts who would assemble them themselves.

Herbst set up shop early in 1965 near his home in Torrance, rented factory space a few months later, hired a handful of draughtsmen and designers, and started work on the infinitude of details that go into the design of any aircraft. A little less than three years later, the work was, by Herbst's estimate, about half done. He'd completed designs for the hull, the cabin superstructure, the doors and the engine loft, and actually built the parts that made up the rear half of the fuselage, put them together, then dismantled them for storage. He'd completed preliminary designs for most other components, built a mock-up of the main landing gear, and completed buoyancy tests that satisfied him that the plane, if it ever got built, would indeed float.

By this time, however, Spencer had lost interest in the project — he'd got involved in designing a homebuilt of his own — and Dent's company, whose profits had financed three years of painstaking work, suddenly found itself in the middle of a bad year, due to a Boeing slowdown. There was no more money available for the Trigull project. Herbst shut down his shop, stored the drawings and completed parts in his own garage, and went back to work for Aeronca.

There was no question in Herbst's mind, though, of abandoning the project. "It's like having a sick elephant in your living room," he once explained. "The only thing you *can't* do is ignore it." Dent hadn't given up either. He was busy with Tyee, but he spent his spare time trying to interest someone, anyone, in reviving the project. One weekend in 1969 he flew to Vancouver and spoke at a meeting of the Vancouver Seabee Club, a highly informal organization with about a dozen members. Two of them were Dave Hazlewood and Paddy Newton.

Newton has been hooked on flying nearly all his life. He joined the Royal Air Force at 16, spent five years with the RAF's Transport Command in the Far East, where he piloted Liberators and C-47s around India and neighboring areas. He finished the war in Singapore, came in 1947 to visit a brother in Vancouver, a city he'd left at the age of six, when his family moved to Belfast. This time he stayed. Three years later he bought his first Seabee, and became the first flying salesman on the B.C. coast. His line was dry goods — needles, thread, blankets, what do you need? The arrival of Newton and his Seabee became an event to anticipate in isolated logging and fishing settlements all along the B.C. coast, as far north as Alaska. In 1957 he went into the mutual funds business, and found the principles were pretty much the same as in selling needles and thread. Within a few years, Newton had written $4 million worth of business for United Investment Services. As the firm's resident vice-president in B.C., he had 500 salesmen working for him in the late 1960s, back in those dimly remembered days when mutual funds were considered a red-hot investment vehicle. Like all good salesmen, he found that many of his clients became his friends, and many of those friends had money to spare. He is a youthful-looking man who wears suede sports jackets in the summer and a Hawaiian tan in the winter. He owns two airplanes and a cherry-red Jensen-Healey, and he seems to know everybody of substance in Vancouver. He'd become friends with Hazlewood through the Seabee Club. "Dave was a very useful guy," says Newton. "He always seemed to have a lot of Seabee spare parts. As a matter of fact, after we got to know each other, he became a substantial shareholder in our mutual fund."

Hazlewood's career has been quieter. He is one of those hardworking, unflamboyant people who win their points not through charm, but through a sort of dogged, inescapable common sense. Too young for the war, he spent eight volunteer years as a parttime militia lieutenant in the Royal Canadian Artillery. Two legacies of that period are a crewcut and a quiet air of command. Mao has written that the great leaders are almost invisible to their followers, and this seems like a fair description of Hazlewood's management style. He's an electrical engineer by training, and he seems to understand instinctively how the talents and strengths of different individuals can be fitted together to produce a team that gets a job done — in much the same way, in fact, as 15,000 separate parts can be fitted together to create a machine that will fly.

All his savvy about airplanes was acquired in his spare time. After graduation from the University of B.C. in 1947, he spent 10 uneventful years as a gas utilization engineer for B.C. Electric, and another eight as staff engineer for Lochhead-Haggerty, a Vancouver firm that designs and builds industrial heat-process equipment. In those 18 years of salaried employment, Hazlewood learned a lot about how things get made in an industrial society. He also learned that "you just can't make it as a salaried employee. You've got to have something of your own." In a small way, he became an entrepreneur in 1958. People, little old ladies mostly, were always calling at Lochhead-Haggerty, he noticed, to buy new heating elements for their pottery kilns. In talking to these $3.98 customers, Hazlewood discovered a small commercial vacuum: in a city that's always had a disproportionate share of potters, there was no pottery supply house. Hazlewood and his wife decided to fill the vacuum with a mail-order business run from their own basement. A few years later, after it was profitable in a small way, they formed another company, Arbutus Ceramic Equipment, to manufacture potters' kilns and wheels.

Ceramics was never more than a sideline, but it gave Hazlewood a taste for risk and reward. In 1965, he and two partners put up $20,000 each to buy a small company called Pacific Controls Ltd., which sold and overhauled thermostats and industrial controls. Hazlewood went into the deal with large expectations. A year later he was sadder and wiser, but at least no poorer. It wasn't an especially profitable business, and there had been policy disagreements with the other operating partner. Hazlewood sold out for about what he'd paid in: "It was a very sad day when I left. I had a lot of dreams."

He spent the next six months Looking Around — not for another job, but for another deal. "Once you've worked for yourself, you're loathe to go back to a nine-to-five job," he says. By this time, he had his eye on something, anything, in the aviation business. He explored the idea of setting up an aircraft-engine overhaul firm. But in the end he went back into the controls business, in direct competition with the firm he'd just left. This time, his partner was a firm that wanted to develop a certain segment of the industrial controls market. Instead of hiring Hazlewood as a salesman, he paid $20,000 for a half interest in a subsidiary company, a corporate device designed to let him run his own show. It wasn't easy. "They were two of the hardest years of my life," he says. And at the end of them, the parent company decided to reorganize its sales structure, which meant re-absorption of Hazlewood's subsidiary into the parent company. Hazlewood didn't want to be anybody's employee, so he sold out once again — this time for a $20,000 profit, which he promptly invested in mutual funds, which promptly declined to approximately nowhere. Dave Hazlewood was 44 and, for all practical purposes, flat broke. He cut his family living expenses to $400 a month, which was about what the ceramics business paid, and, once again, started Looking Around. He had a wife, a baby daughter and a Seabee to support. His lifestyle, he says, "wasn't too different from welfare."

In September 1969, he and Paddy Newton attended the joint meeting of the Vancouver and Seattle Seabee Clubs, where Bob Dent outlined his thwarted plans for a new amphibian. To a man with no job, no prospects and a yearning to get into the aviation business, it sounded interesting. In November, Hazlewood and Newton flew to Everett and, after a few hours discussion, agreed to pay Tyee Aircraft $1,000 for an option to buy the Trigull project for $135,000. Later, they flew to Torrance to see Chuck Herbst, and for the first time set eyes on what was to become the Trigull. "It was a bunch of drawings and a few dusty aircraft parts," says Newton, "all stacked up in Chuck's garage." Herbst, who was still nursing his dream, quickly agreed to join the design team, if Newton and Hazlewood could raise the money.

What they were selling, at this point, were two factors in an incomplete equation: the unfinished Trigull project, and the fact that the Canadian federal government, after closing down Air Canada's overhaul facilities in Winnipeg, had indicated that it would support new aviation businesses that moved in to fill the gap in Western Canada. Although the bloom was fading fast from the stock market, junior industrial issues were still coming onto the market in Vancouver, often selling briskly. "It was still the euphoric time when you could sell anything," says Hazlewood.

"But hell, we didn't know what we were talking about. All we had was a pipe dream with a dozen pages of writing. There was nothing real about it — just some unfinished drawings of an unfinished airplane." They didn't realize it at the time, but something was missing from their equation — some element of solidity that would make their scheme more than an expression of hope.

And so Hazlewood spent six months "knocking on the door of every fancy office in Vancouver. I was the one who had the time, and I'd got myself into a position where I could go for an extended period without going under. I wasn't buying new clothes and I wasn't making any changes to the house." Hazlewood must have talked to most of the promoters, brokers, entrepreneurs and old-money people within a two-mile radius of Howe Street, but he got precisely nowhere. "It was discouraging, but it was interesting too."

The breakthrough came in February 1970, when Hazlewood, at Newton's suggestion, went to see Don Cameron, president of Canadian Aircraft Products Ltd. CAPL, the product of an early-1960s merger of two small Vancouver aviation firms, has about 70 employees, and grosses about $1 million annually on various subcontracting chores for DeHavilland, Douglas and Canadair. CAPL makes the floats for the DeHavilland Twin Otter — the largest floats being made anywhere — and also manufactures part of the tail assembly for the Douglas DC-9. Hazlewood says he went to Cameron mainly for advice, for his efforts at raising money were getting nowhere. But Cameron showed immediate interest: it was one of those sweet situations where the separate interests of two parties mesh perfectly. "Dave had a project and needed a place to carry it out," says Cameron. "We had a plant and were looking for additional projects. It was a natural. So we contracted with each other to join forces."

Under the contract, CAPL agreed to build the Trigull in its own plant in Richmond, B.C., and to take one third of its direct labor costs in Trident shares, instead of cash. By the time the plane flew, CAPL owned 30 percent of Trident's shares, making it by far the largest single shareholder. Instead of taking $135,000 cash for the uncompleted plane, Tyee Aircraft took half that amount in Trident shares, and the other half in the form of a five-year note which could, at Tyee's option, be converted into shares.

48

CAPL's expertise, and the fact that it was an ongoing manufacturing business, made it possible to nail down the final factor in the equation: federal government support. Early in March 1970, Trident applied for a $400,000 grant from the Department of Industry, Trade and Commerce's Program for the Advancement of Industrial Technology (PAIT).

The PAIT grant was finally approved in the spring of 1971, and work on the plane began in CAPL's plant. Meanwhile, Newton and Hazlewood kept visiting people's offices, trying to sell shares to individual investors. They raised money from friends, relatives, friends-of-friends, aviation enthusiasts and a mechanic who, says Hazlewood, "just happened to wander in off the street one day." As the work proceeded, they discovered what they'd bought was much less than half a completed airplane. The trouble was that what Herbst had already designed were components for what would have been a hand-crafted, one-of-a-kind machine. To build a plane that would not only fly, but could be mass-produced, considerable redesign was needed — especially on the nose wheel and the wing, which had to be altered to meet new specifications of the U.S. Federal Aviation Administration.

The plane cost an even $1 million to develop to the flying stage. Trident had to go back to Ottawa for an extension of its PAIT grant, and also received a $125,000 grant under the federal Industrial Research and Development Incentives Act (IRDIA). By early 1975, the plane had cost $2.2 million to develop, and about $1,350,000 of this sum came from the federal government which, even if the plane were to become a commercial success, would own nary a rivet on the Trigull's glossy hull.

Five days before the first test flight, Chuck Herbst and Paul Hartman were leaning over a designer's drawing board, peering at the operations manual for the Trigull's propeller. It's a Hartzell reversible propeller, a small miracle of technology in itself. A governor actuates a piston, and changes the angle of the blades at certain speeds, thus automatically braking the plane during landings. Designer and test pilot were talking about how the thing works, and how to deal with it during the test flight, using that unearthly

49

jargon that only experienced pilots understand. They talked of "coarsening the blade," and "overspeed," and "full fine position" — engineers' talk that is incomprehensible to outsiders. But even an outsider could glimpse a certain closeness in the way they talked. Both men had worked themselves into a position of near-communion with the machine. Hartman had driven out from Ottawa a month earlier, and since then he'd been living in a trailer parked outside the Canadian Aircraft Products building, no further than 50 feet from where his plane sat. By now he knew every part of the plane, almost as well as Herbst did himself. An odd craftsman's intimacy had grown up between them.

Tony Quick, an Englishman who would not look out of character with an RAF silk scarf knotted carelessly at his throat, is explaining the .8 learning curve to a visitor. He started servicing P-40s and Spitfires when he was 17, and now he's the manufacturing manager for Canadian Aircraft Products Ltd. — which means, in effect, that he constitutes a one-man loyal opposition to the engineers who are trying to make the Trigull the most perfect plane imaginable.

"This prototype will have taken roughly 8,000 man-hours by the time it flies. Well, the .8 learning curve is based on experience in the industry — that people learn as they go along, so it only takes 80 percent as long to build the second airplane as it did to build the first. And only 80 percent as long to build the third as it took to build the second. Production control is based on coming down that curve properly. You stand or fall on this type of exercise. According to the learning curve, it should only take 1,800 or 2,000 man-hours to build the Trigull. But we won't hit that until the 75th airplane. If we don't, we're in trouble."

Quick's interest in the Trigull has been to make sure that each part that comes off the drawing boards can be manufactured by the hundreds, within pre-set cost limits. "Designers, being perfectionists, like very close tolerances. They like things to *fit*. The trouble is, the closer your tolerances, the higher your costs. So, if we find a design that's high in man-hours, we've got to protest it. The war is continuous. It never stops."

The Trigull's first test flight is scheduled for the coming weekend, but Quick isn't too excited at the prospect. He knows the plane will fly. But he has many intricate charts on his office wall that reflect his longer-range preoccupation: will it fly on the assembly line?

Yes, the Trigull will fly. But will it sell? Pilots are a notoriously conservative species and, when a new aircraft comes on the market, the word of mouth bandied around airstrips across the continent can be swift and devastating. Or it can be favorable. Newton and Hazlewood spent several painstaking weeks pondering this question, before they signed the deal with Dent and Herbst. They concluded that the Trigull, if it performed to specifications, would be unlike any other aircraft being manufactured anywhere in the world; that there was no aircraft available with performance and capabilities sufficiently similar to be deemed "competition"; and that a sales goal of 50 airplanes a year, once full production had been achieved, was a realistic and perhaps conservative estimate.

The Trigull was designed to sell "in the high 50s" — perhaps as much as $60,000 with a heavy load of accessories. This is roughly the price range of the most popular light amphibian sold today, the amphibious float-equipped Cessna 185. But the Trigull will fly faster, stall at a slower speed (48 miles per hour), perform better in rough water, carry more passengers and a larger payload, and sell for about $9,000 less than the float-equipped Cessna. "If the plane performs the way it's supposed to," says Newton, "we have no worries about sales."

Six months before they went into the deal, Newton and Hazlewood sent descriptive brochures to all air charter operators in Canada, and received replies indicating interest from most of them. On the basis of this "survey," they concluded that a potential market exists in Canada, among commercial operators alone, for 110 planes.

Using this nugget of information, they extrapolated. They assumed that the U.S. light aircraft market is 12 times the size of Canada's, but also assumed that the U.S. interest would be one third of the Canadian interest. That makes another 440 planes.

They also assumed a market potential of another 110 planes among sports and corporate customers in Canada, and multipled by 12 to get the comparable U.S. figure. Grand total: 1,980 planes.

Of course this is the purest guesswork. Everything depends on how well the plane performs, and how energetically it's marketed. Trident's plan is to sell direct from the factory initially, then appoint dealers around the continent. In 1969, some 15,000 light aircraft were sold in the U.S., for a total price of around $500 million. Trident estimates that if it can grab off only .34 percent of this market, it's in business.

Estimates like these, of course, are compiled mainly to reassure the sort of investor who likes to be reassured by market surveys. In fact, Newton and Hazlewood are operating on what may be the most reliable sales indicator available at an early stage: their gut feeling, as experienced pilots of amphibious light aircraft, that the Trigull is a plane they'd like to own, and everyone they know would like to own too. Early interest in the plane seems to confirm their hunch. Long before the first test flight, Trident had received more than 200 letters of enquiry from people who'd seen articles about the plane in aviation magazines. Two customers had actually put down $5,000 deposits, and 20 others had "reserved serial numbers" — which isn't as firm as a deposit, but is considered to be better than a letter of intent.

When the Trigull taxied its first 100 feet across the tarmac, a Seabee, by purest coincidence, just happened to be taxiing nearby, on its way to the hangar next door. Don Cameron, president of CAPL, looked at the Trigull rolling across the runway, then looked at the old Seabee. "Eat your heart out!" he yelled at the pilot. Then he laughed.

The day before the first test flight, a Saturday, the Trigull almost got off the ground. Dark clouds were massing over the mountains to the north as Hartman taxied the plane along a main runway, seeing how it performed at various ground speeds. Chuck Herbst and a few colleagues paced him along the runway in a yellow pick-up truck. As the plane skimmed along the tarmac, you could see Hartman through the cockpit window. Beneath his white crash helmet the experienced pilot was grinning like a kid.

Nearly 50 people — mechanics, shareholders, wives, girl friends, children, Ministry of Transport officials, a few newsmen, even a couple of dogs — had been waiting since early morning to see the Trigull fly. While he was waiting, Paddy Newton polished his red Jensen-Healey. Hazlewood prowled along the sidelines, a weird, private grin on his face. Mechanics tinkered endlessly with the engine and cockpit controls, and it wasn't until late afternoon that Hartman pronounced himself ready for taxi tests. The weather had cleared a little since morning. Everyone was hoping that Hartman might decide the plane felt right, push the throttle forward an extra inch and leap into the air. Most of the spectators were standing on a series of tall, grassy mounds that lined the runway. During the war they were camouflaged storage bins for bombs, and now they made a perfect vantage-point to watch the Trigull, representing years of dreams and thousands of man-hours and, at this point in its development, nearly $1 million of other people's money, as it barreled westward along the runway until it was almost out of sight.

Chuck Herbst was driving the pick-up truck almost in the shadow of the plane's wing, as Hartman turned around at the end of the runway and started his run back to the hangar. Halfway there, the plane picked up speed, started pulling away from the pick-up truck. Someone in the back of the truck shouted "Nose-wheel up!" — and sure enough, the plane was racing along at 65 miles per hour on the two wheels of its main gear. Only another breath would carry it into the air.

But Hartman kept the speed steady and stayed on the ground. Then, far ahead of the pick-up truck, the plane abruptly slowed and stopped. "Shit," said Herbst. As the truck pulled alongside the stalled plane, Hartman opened the cockpit door and grinned at Herbst. "Anyone got a dipstick?" he said. Inexplicably, the motor had shut down. Later they discovered it was caused by some malfunction of the fuel pump. "Lucky it happened on the ground," someone said.

In the life history of a new airplane, the first test flight is of only symbolic significance. All the important decisions are made months and years earlier, on the drawing boards, in the wind tunnel, on the factory floor. Inspectors from the Ministry of Transport had been installed at the plant for months, like rabbis in a kosher slaughterhouse, ensuring that each part, as it came out of the machine shop, conformed to its written specifications. A ministry man had gone over the plane for days prior to the day of the test flight, checking its innards as carefully as Hartman did himself.

Once the plane had flown, Dave Hazlewood told a visitor a few days before the flight, then the real work begins. It would take months to obtain federal certification — the Canadian government's painstaking assurance that the plane was safe to fly.

"The financial people get all hung up on certification, but really, it's only an exercise. The Ministry of Transport doesn't care if a plane is salable — just that it's safe. Once that plane flies, then my real problems begin. It's a mountain still ahead of me. Once it flies, it means I've got a shop full of people standing around waiting for me to raise $2 million so they can start manufacturing. And we can't start chasing the next batch of money until the financial community is convinced the thing will actually fly. That's why I can't share all this enthusiasm about the test flight – because I know that once that plane's in the air, I've got a serious problem."

The mechanics have been tinkering with the engines all morning, as the same assembly of wives, shareholders, dogs, newsmen and assorted well-wishers stand around in front of the Harrison Airways hangar, waiting for that moment when all three wheels leave the ground.

It's a little after three in the afternoon now, and Hartman, finally, is ready to go. He has a parachute strapped to his back and, on the cockpit floor beside his seat, he's placed an inflatable Mae West life preserver in a plastic bag. The technicians have installed a special lever beside his left hand. If there's sudden trouble, all Hartman has to do is bang that lever, and the port door will fall off. A CBC cameraman has arranged to be flying above the runway — in a Seabee, appropriately — as the Trigull takes off. "This one could change from a public-affairs item to a spot news item in one hell of a hurry," the cameraman tells one of his colleagues.

Dave Hazlewood is pacing around, mostly on the sidelines, a movie camera in his hand and that same private grin on his face. One of the people from CAPL calls out to him: "Dave, we've decided we're going to call an obstetrician to look after you." He looks calm but he is all knots inside. A camera shutter clicks behind his back as the plane is being fueled, and Hazlewood jumps visibly, then looks embarrassed. "I thought I heard somebody striking a match," he says.

Fueling completed, seven men push the Trigull away from the hangar, into a clear space on the tarmac. Hartman turns on the starter. We hear that electric whine for 16 seconds as the propeller slowly revolves, then stops. Chuck Herbst walks forward, about to shout something to Hartman through the window. But Hartman just nods and tries again. This time the motor starts, a lovely sound. The time is 3:22. Paddy Newton beams. "Have you ever heard a motor that sounds like that?" he says.

Hazlewood is watching from a grassy mound along the runway as the Trigull taxis along Runway 12 prior to takeoff. Newton is going to observe the event from above, piloting his own Seabee, with the CBC cameraman in the passenger seat. Herbst has the best spot of all. He's been ferried out to the runway in a radio-equipped station wagon, and he's standing halfway down Runway 12, camera at the ready, at the point where the Trigull is expected to leave the ground. The plane is a faint speck down at the far end of the runway. Then, a second later, the speck grows larger and he can hear the motor getting louder.

It's almost an anticlimax. The Trigull zooms past Herbst, its nose wheel spinning in the air, looking clean and ready and then . . . yes it's off the ground, it's aloft, it's into the air and already it's a disappearing object in the sky. The landing gear retracts as it goes. Herbst watches his plane. He looks almost disappointed, for at this moment it doesn't feel like an old dream made flesh. It just looked like — well, like a light aircraft making a takeoff, something that happens every few minutes at every large airport. "Well, it's going, eh?" he says.

Herbst looks at his feet, then looks at the sky. There are two specks up there. The one in front is the Trigull. The one behind is

Newton's Seabee, following the newborn plane, trying to photograph its flight. "See the Seabee?" says Herbst. "It's not closing on him. The Seabee's no good as a chase plane. It's like the turtle and the hare. Look at him . . ."

Then it hits him. That's *his* plane up there, a machine that grew out of his brains and 10 years of his life and, Jesus, it's leaving the Seabee behind, it's so *fast* . . .

Out here in the middle of the airfield, the swallows act strange. They flip around close to the ground, darting closer to people than birds normally do. And a swallow flits past Chuck Herbst's head as the enormity of his own plane being up there dawns on him. And he stands there in the wind, stands in this funny posture on one foot, his arms outstretched, looking at the sky and laughing, laughing with a kind of pure wild glee I'd never heard in a man's laugh before.

Footnote: The Trigull performed beautifully in the succeeding phases of its testing program. It climbed to 25,000 feet, setting a world altitude record for planes of its class, and exceeded its estimated cruising speed of 166 miles per hour. "Experience is showing," Chuck Herbst told the Vancouver Sun, "that we are likely to have about a 10 percent appreciation on some of our [performance] targets."

By early 1975, the project still wasn't off the ground. They'd built and flown a second prototype, this one equipped with a smaller engine from the same family. They'd received further development loans from the B.C. Development Corp. and the Industrial Development Bank. In March 1975, Hazlewood was still busy doing what he'd been doing since 1969: hunting for money. He was working on a deal whereby the federal Department of Industry, Trade and Commerce would guarantee $2 million worth of loans, and the Industrial Development Bank and the B.C. Development Corp. would guarantee another $1 million. These guarantees would be contingent on Trident raising another $750,000 worth of equity. "Ten minutes after we get the money," said Hazlewood, "we'll go into production."

It didn't happen that way. Ottawa came through with an offer for a $2-million loan guarantee, but the strings attached to the offer made it almost impossible, in Hazlewood's view, to attract the remaining capital from other sources. On April 1, 1975, Trident Aircraft shut down its operations and laid off 12 employees. Hazlewood called it "voluntary dormancy to prevent bankruptcy." When reporters called to enquire as to the fate of the company, it was Hazlewood who answered the phone himself. The day the firm shut down, the company had 83 deposits from serious potential purchasers.

And so we have a cliff-hanging finale for the story of Trident Aircraft. A few men with a dream and a lot of guts built an airplane, an airplane that not only flew, but attracted enough market interest virtually to guarantee the first 18 months of profitable production. And still they couldn't find the money. By the time you read this, the company may be dead, or it may happily be building airplanes. "I can only be optimistic," Hazlewood told me. "I have no choice."

57

4

PHIL JAPP:
FROM ASSEMBLY LINE
TO FIRING LINE

Phil Japp didn't look much like an entrepreneur that day. He looked exactly like a man who'd spent the morning wrestling heavy machinery around a bare concrete floor, and nailing up wallboard in a cubicle that would someday be his office, and connecting steam pipes and shifting heavy barrels that were full to the brim of rubber stampings that looked like miniature hockey pucks. He was tired and grimy and a little punchy. For the last two weeks, he'd been working 16 to 18 hours a day, installing machinery in a building on Toronto's Danforth Avenue that was tucked away behind a transmission repair shop. The first time Japp had seen the inside of that building was in 1938 when, as an 11-year-old kid, he'd spent a few weeks as a milkman's helper. The building was a dairy then. And when Japp moved in with his machinery 36 years later, in February 1974, the iron rings where they'd once tethered the horses were still mounted along one brick wall. Upstairs was another large, bare room, now filled with more miscellaneous bits of machinery, iron moulds used for retreading tires, and stacks of rubber rolls. Somehow, within another week of 18-hour days, Japp had to wrestle all the elements he'd assembled — the rubber forms, the machinery, the huge vulcanizing oven almost the size of a locomotive, with a sliding door that weighed more than three tons — into something alive: a functioning plant where rubber could be stamped, vulcanized, moulded, cured and grafted to the inside of various containers, from swimming pools to vats for storing sulphuric acid.

58

In the trade, such places are known as lining shops. There are about half a dozen of them in Ontario. Japp had spent more than half his life working with rubber, mostly on the assembly line at Dunlop Canada Ltd.'s big Toronto plant. But now he was working for himself. He had a piece of paper in his pocket which said that if he could turn this machinery-strewn junkyard into a profitable lining shop, he'd own the business within two years. "The place is a goddam mess right now," he told a visitor, "but by next week it's going to be operating. It may not look like much to you, but it gets *my* adrenalin flowing." Japp was out to build something out of nothing, and he liked the feeling. The entrepreneurial urge is not restricted to men with clean fingernails.

Phil Japp's story is this: he quit school at 14, and at 16 got a job in Dunlop's dark, satanic factory on Queen Street East, not far from where he'd grown up. He married at 19 and stayed at Dunlop for 26 years, a working stiff in an assembly-line job. Almost certainly, he would have stayed there until he turned 65, then retired on an adequate pension. But in 1970, Dunlop decided to shut down the ancient plant, which meant instant unemployment for most of its 600 employees. Japp, who was president of his union when the shutdown happened, found himself shoved into public prominence. The closure — of a foreign-controlled plant, accomplished without a murmur of protest from the headquarters of an American-controlled union — became a *cause celebre* in the media. And Japp, who staged demonstrations at the Legislature, debated in a TV studio with the Prime Minister, and haggled with company officials over pension and severance benefits for the men, found himself in the middle of it.

It was the most remarkable thing that had ever happened to him. And when it was over, Japp and four of his fellow workers borrowed $35,000 from the Ontario Development Corp., bought machinery from their former employer, and went into business as Porta-Flex Products Ltd., manufacturing rubber handrails for escalators.

In less than two years, Porta-Flex had done $1 million worth of business, and was a solid commercial success. But Japp, partly through disagreements with his partners, partly through a restless urge to try something else, sold out his interest. He paid $4,000 for control of a small company called Great Eastern Linings that made vinyl linings for swimming pools. Great Eastern also did subcontracting work for a lining shop owned by Tip Top Products Ltd. The lining shop was losing money and had to move from its location in Ajax, Ontario, so Tip Top's owner made Japp an offer: move the operation within a month and make it pay within two years, and the company is yours. Japp accepted, and started work on his third entrepreneurial venture in five years.

But what happened to Phil Japp's job is much less interesting than what happened to Phil Japp's head. Working in a large factory can be a self-imposed term of imprisonment, in a relatively comfortable cage. Suddenly, one day, the cage wasn't there any more. And Japp, at the age of 43, suddenly experienced a world he'd only read about in the newspapers — a world of politicians, media people, TV cameras, long lunches, strategies and, yes, decisions. Forced out of an environment of relative security, he decided to live in an environment of risk. Almost everything about him changed: the way he looked, how he dressed, what he ate for lunch, the hours he worked, the worries that kept him awake at night, his friends, the size of his dreams, his income. After half a lifetime as a member of what is no longer referred to in this country as The Working Class, he became a small businessman, a member of what we might as well call The Middle Class.

In many ways, it was a painful transition. Some of the time, as all those changes reshuffled his life, Japp felt like a traitor to his own origins. But most of the time, he felt like himself, only more so: learning and growing in a dozen different directions, discovering, with an impact that few men in this country have felt, the difference between working in the hold of a large freighter, and steering your own small boat across an ocean.

Many Canadians fondly assume that they live in a relatively classless society. But what happened to Phil Japp shows that a class system does exist, and shows something of how it works. It is not a system based on rank and privilege and inheritance. But the labor force in this country is still divided, and quite rigidly, into people who are using and developing most of their talents, and people who are not — into those who hate their jobs and those who love them. Japp's story doesn't necessarily validate the middle-class myth that "anybody can make it if they try." But it does demonstrate that the industrial system, when it uses people merely as extensions of machines, is squandering a precious resource: the ingenuity and ambitions and dreams of many human beings.

There is an honorable working-class tradition in Toronto: street after street of tiny, well-kept houses, some of them a century old; the homes of Anglo-Saxon families who attended church, paid their bills, honored the King, fought in his wars and, when the factories were open, worked in factories. Unionism is a part of this tradition. So, strangely enough, is Toryism. Phil Japp's father and mother were part of this tradition. The father was a shoe-cutter, and proud of his trade. But between 1929 and 1939, like most of his neighbors, he was unemployed, broke and on the dole. In those days, even when three quarters of the families on your street were "on the pogey," it wasn't something you bragged about. Poverty was something you blamed yourself for, something you tried to conceal.

Japp was only seven or eight when he first accompanied his father down to the welfare office, where they had a separate line for veterans, and where the handouts consisted not of money, but of cardboard boxes containing staples such as peanut butter, dried white beans, tea and lard. In those days, poor kids in Toronto wore what amounted to a school uniform: black bulky-knit sweaters with turned-up collars and an orange stripe on the sleeve. "Pogey sweaters," they were called. They came at Christmas in the food hampers sent by The Toronto Star. At Morse Street Public School roughly half the kids in the schoolyard seemed to be wearing The Star's pogey sweaters. "I felt acutely the lack of money," Japp recalled years afterward. "I felt acutely the lack of material things. I even used to lie to the other kids on my street about what I had. They lied to me too. But we all wore those pogey sweaters. It hurt. Don't kid yourself. It hurt — did me, anyway."

At 14, he quit school, and got a job in a cork factory. The pay was low, but the plant employed a lot of girls. He didn't like the job, and he quit. At 16, in April 1944, he started work at Dunlop, and the old building on Queen Street became his world for the next 26 years. From 1947 to 1958, he made conveyor belts. "There isn't much to it, except reading the specifications. You work on a 37-foot table. First you pull rolls of rubber and fabric from overhead spools, lay them on top of one another, make a sandwich out of them, then feed them through rollers onto a wind-up device. You'd walk up and down that goddam table incessantly. We figured that for every 37 feet of belting we made, you had to walk about 400 feet. I did that for 10 years. *Ten years!* There were some variations, but basically it was the same operation over and over again. I once did the whole operation with my eyes shut, just to see if I could do it."

Dunlop workers were paid a base rate, with extra pay for extra production. It meant that most of the men worked fast and hard. "If you'd wanted to live on your base rate, which was your guaranteed earnings, the groceries would have been few and far between," says Japp. "With those incentive rates, you pushed and pushed and pushed like a sonofabitch — and you became . . . well, you almost left the human race. You'd get so involved in trying to beat that goddam clock. You'd be resentful about taking lunch breaks. You'd even resent going to the goddam bathroom. I'm sure chronic constipation must go hand-in-glove with incentive rates. Sometimes I'd walk out of that place so tired I could hardly put one foot ahead of the other."

Any energy, any ingenuity that remained was channeled into pranks, some of them quite funny. The pranks are what the men who worked at Dunlop usually recall. Once, Japp and a pal connected a plastic water pipe to the navel of a Playboy fold-out that someone had pinned to a bulletin board. Whenever anyone stopped for a searching examination of her anatomy, Japp stepped on a rubber bulb, and the art lover got a squirt of water in the eye. Hilarious.

Japp: "There was this machine about 40 feet from us, across the room. It had a trip-wire running down the side. We got some nylon fishing filament, ran it down a hole in the floor to the basement, across some water pipes, up through another hole near this machine. Then we tied it to the trip-wire. Then we went back to the other end, tied a loop on it so that, by pulling my foot up, I could stop the machine 40 feet away from me. We played with that for about three hours. 'Harvey,' we'd yell, 'your machine's gonna stop.' And it did. Harvey was just about going out of his stick."

There was also the dummy that some night-shift jokers rigged up in a washroom cubicle, complete with trousers and shoes, which were conspicuously visible below the cubicle's door. Bombing was another occasional diversion. You filled a lunch bag with carbon black, leaned out a window, and aimed it at one of your colleagues who was working in the yard below. With any luck at all, your man was enveloped in a sooty, black cloud.

"This one day," said Japp, "this guy's got a small bag of lamp black, and he drops it into the yard right beside one of his friends. He happens to look over to the side of the yard and, holy Christ, here's the president of the company, old J. I. Simpson, standing there, looking up at him, watching the whole scene!

"Well, this guy ran like a sonofabitch, straight to the bathroom, borrowed a razor from a foreman, shaved off his moustache and put on a goddam sweater and hat! Old Simpson went up those stairs like a shot looking for him. But he never found him."

Like prisoners, everyone at Dunlop had escape routes and escape fantasies. The cottage, the two-week vacation, hobbies, drinking, anything. And always, year after year, they talked about quitting. Japp: "My pal on the belt-making table was Clell Maracle, and he had one ambition. To get out. He told me. He'd say, 'I'll work here until I'm ready, and then I'll quit.' Every year I'd tell him, 'Clell, you're full of shit.' But in the 20th year he said, 'Yeah? You think so?' And he *did* quit. He had some property on the Mohawk reserve in Deseronto, and he built a big house on it. Clell got out, but it took him 20 years."

But most stayed. "The big thing I used to notice," says Japp, "was the goddam calendars. As soon as a guy's holiday was over, he'd start crossing off the days until the next one — so many days, so many weeks to holiday time."

Japp had escape fantasies too. He'd quit and go farming. He'd quit and start a garage with his brother-in-law. He'd set up as an independent operator, doing on-site repairs of conveyor belts. As he became increasingly active in Local 132 of the United Rubber,

Cork, Linoleum & Plastic Workers Union, he began to see promotion within the union as an escape route too — a field organizer, maybe, or a district representative.

But mostly it was just locker-room talk, these dreams of escape. Dunlop's workers were better-paid than the industry average. The work was hard, but there were plenty of worse ways to make a living. Japp knew there was a big world waiting outside the plant. But when you work rotating shifts — days one week, afternoons the next, nights the week after that — for more than a decade, you don't get to see much of it. Practically the only people he ever saw were his family — his wife Lorraine and two daughters — his neighbors and the men in the plant.

One year, Japp noticed a couple of surprising things. At home, his daughters had somehow turned into teen-agers. And at the plant, he started noticing a conversational shift among the men his own age. "For years, these guys had been talking about 'What I'm going to do when I quit.' And now, suddenly, they were talking about 'What I am going to do when I get my pension.' Holy Christ! By that time I was fairly active in the union, and I knew by reading the statistics that you're not going to do a hell of a lot when you get your pension, because you're not going to live that long. That used to bother me. It bothered me a lot."

Japp didn't know it then, but he wasn't going to get his pension. Dunlop's Industrial Rubber Goods Division, based at the Queen Street plant, was in trouble, and had been for at least a decade. Rising costs, competition from foreign suppliers and from alternate materials, such as plastics, had steadily narrowed the company's options. In 1965, Firestone had closed its plant in Lindsay, Ontario; and that was only one symptom of a malaise that affected the entire industry. By 1969, foreign firms were supplying about 27 percent of the industrial rubber goods market; a few years earlier, it had been only 12 percent. Late that year, Dunlop submitted a $350,000 bid to supply industrial rubber belting to Ontario Hydro, a bid that left only a minimal profit margin. But a Japanese firm got the contract, with a bid for $270,000. "Our prices are no longer being set according to our own cost structures," Dunlop's Canadian president, George Plummer, told the newspapers, "but rather by the lowest efficient producers in other countries who wish to invade our markets."

The men in the plant didn't know it, but large decisions were being made that would affect their futures. Late in 1968, Dunlop had appointed a three-man task force under vice-president E. C. Markwick to make a wide-ranging study of the industrial rubber goods market in Canada, and figure out ways to survive in it. Markwick's conclusions, in mid-1969, consisted of a series of options, ranging from business-as-usual to immediate closure, and predictions on how each option might affect profitability. Management chose a course that became known as Plan C — a drastic reduction in the number of product lines and ruthless cost-cutting. The best the company could hope for under Plan C was marginal profitability within three years.

But by the end of 1969, it had become apparent that even Plan C wasn't going to work. Sales were running 25 percent below the anticipated level and losses had increased. And so, after a six-month trial of Plan C, management made the decision it had been trying to avoid for years: the Queen Street plant would close on May 1, 1970. In February, Dunlop executives flew to Ottawa to quietly inform the federal government and, the following day, passed the word to Stanley Randall, then Ontario's minister of trade and development. "With hindsight," one Dunlop executive said, "I can see that we never even should have started Plan C. The chances of success were so remote. We were probably over-optimistic in even trying it, but we did our ruddy damnedest to keep the ruddy thing going."

For months, Japp had suspected that something was up. There'd been talk of modernizing the plant, but the promised new machines failed to arrive. And, at a dinner for 25-year Dunlop employees which he'd attended, company executives had predicted great things for other divisions of the company but, interestingly, hadn't uttered a word about the Queen Street plant.

And so, on the morning of March 6, 1970, Japp and the heads of two other unions were called into the office of Frank Churcher, the industrial relations manager, and handed a mimeographed announcement of the closure. At the same moment, a fleet of taxis was dashing all over Toronto, delivering secretly prepared press releases to newspaper offices and radio stations.

Japp's immediate reaction, as president of the union, was to fight. "When it first started," he says, "I didn't know what I was going to do from one day to the next. I thought the company might bow to the old pressure play, the way they'd done in contract negotiations in the old days. I didn't realize that this time it was a different ball game."

It was a publicity war without a war aim. If he'd stopped to think about it, Japp now concedes, he probably would have concluded that a protest was hopeless. But his visceral reaction was to fight, to protest, to generate as many headlines and raise as much stink as possible. The union paid his wages for the next seven weeks, while Japp did exactly that.

Almost as a matter of routine, the union fired off protest telegrams to everyone its executive could think of: Prime Minister Trudeau, Ontario's Premier John Robarts, Stanley Randall, Dunlop's chairman in England, the media, everybody. The replies, predictably, were noncomittal. "I understand the feelings of your members," replied Premier Robarts in a brush-off letter, "but I believe that a businessman must have the right to decide what is best for his company."

Japp took to the streets too. Five busloads of Dunlop workers, with a piper, drove to Ottawa and demonstrated with placards on Parliament Hill. About 400 Dunlop workers turned up at a rally in front of the Ontario Legislature. "We feel we must not and will not accept the loss of our jobs without making a protest!" said one of the mimeographed fliers they handed out. The union also circulated a petition that attracted 30,000 signatures protesting the closure.

The publicity was making Japp a mini-celebrity. He discovered the heady experience of going home at night and watching himself being interviewed on the evening news. He debated the closure with Prime Minister Trudeau in a TV studio, but the segment was never broadcast. He was quoted almost daily in the newspapers. At one point he drove to Brantford, Ontario, where Premier Robarts was appearing at a Progressive Conservative rally and, from the audience, directed awkward questions about the closure at the premier.

"He was really polite and civil," said Japp after the encounter, "which is more than I can say for myself. I was pretty excited. But of course he wasn't going to be moved." Japp was discovering a talent he hadn't known he possessed: a flair for publicity. He was quotable; he was articulate; he instinctively understood reporters' need for fresh copy. The petition and the publicity attracted outsiders to the cause. Intellectuals started issuing statements. Melville Watkins, the University of Toronto economist and guru of radical nationalism, interested himself in the closure. University students joined the protest demonstrations. The Dunlop closure came to symbolize for many the extent of this country's reliance on foreign capital, and the control of our destiny we've lost as a result.

As the weeks passed, it became apparent that, although plenty of heat and headlines were being generated, nothing was going to save those 600 jobs. The protests by this time had acquired a focus: the government must pass legislation requiring advance notice for workers in the event of future closures. Japp, in a desperation move, also tried to interest the Ontario government in a feasibility study of a worker-owned plant on Queen Street. Suppose Dunlop's workers invested their severance pay to buy the plant, his reasoning went; couldn't at least some of the jobs be saved that way? The government declined to undertake such a study. Even inside the plant, some of the men felt Japp was fighting a useless battle. An anonymous cartoon pinned on the plant bulletin board showed Japp, with briefcase and horn-rim glasses, gazing at the reeking corpse of a horse and telling his followers: "And I'm telling you guys, that horse is *alive!*"

As the end approached, even Japp began to accept the inevitable. And he found time to be personally frightened about his own future. On the last day of April, there was a meeting at the Ontario Legislature building between two cabinet ministers and various labor spokesmen, including Japp. The meeting lasted an hour, but there was little talk of keeping the plant open. Instead, they discussed relocation, job retraining, how the federal Manpower office could help find the men new jobs. "That's it," Japp told reporters after the meeting. "We've reached the end of the line."

On the final day, May 1, he'd planned to make one last visit to the plant. "I was determined to spend the day there, but I couldn't do it. I talked to maybe six guys, then I choked up. I couldn't hack it. I wasn't the tough guy I thought I was." Japp went home to his tiny house in East Toronto. Nobody was home. He sat alone on a sofa and wept for two hours. Phil Japp was 43, and his 26 years at Dunlop had come to an end.

The peculiar fact about the Dunlop closure — which generated so much concern, so many signatures on petitions, so much public sympathy for the men involved — is that, four years later, the vast majority of those men were happily installed in better jobs. Dunlop's severance benefits, which went beyond what the law demands, and even beyond what was spelled out in union contracts, were large enough to give most of the men a breathing spell. Japp's payment was about $4,000. On top of that there was unemployment insurance. Like most of Dunlop's 600 rejects, Japp could afford at least a few weeks to look around.

Within two weeks, he found himself talking with three of his former work mates about the chances of starting a company of their own. The idea had occurred to them in the hectic weeks between the announcement and the closure, when the notion of a worker-owned plant on Queen Street had been proposed, and then abandoned. Between them, Ray Halliday, Arthur Cross, George Fisher and Japp had a total of 86 years' experience in industrial rubber goods. They knew everything there was to know about the physical process of building conveyer belts, escalator handrails, industrial floormats and the dozens of other products that Dunlop used to make on Queen Street. They also knew that one of the division's few profitable lines was escalator handrails. At Dunlop, they'd often been weeks, even months, behind on their orders. And now Dunlop's big handrail press — there were only seven in North America — was standing idle on Queen Street. Couldn't it be bought and revived in a new location? Wouldn't a profitable handrail company replace at least a few of the jobs that had been lost? The four men had plenty of time to discuss the prospect. After several meetings in each other's living rooms, they decided to go ahead. The more they investigated the deal, the better it looked.

The first step was to see the Ontario Development Corp., a provincial agency that makes loans and grants to companies that will create new jobs in Ontario. Japp and his partners found the ODC's people efficient and helpful. First, they explained some of the ground rules. They'd have to be incorporated. They'd have to demonstrate some hard evidence of what they hoped would happen. They'd need cost and revenue projections. And, the ODC explained, the partners would be expected to put some money of their own into the venture. Each put up $4,000.

Slowly, over the summer, the four men pieced the deal together. Dunlop's management proved to be helpful. The handrail press that would be their major capital asset was available for $35,000, along with all the ancillary equipment. At the ODC's suggestion, they brought in a fifth partner who'd had management experience — Walter Merkel, a Dunlop divisional manager whose job had evaporated when the plant closed. Japp had faced him many times across the bargaining table, and respected him. In Ajax, Ontario, an industrial suburb of Oshawa, they found suitable quarters in a concrete-block building that rented for less than $500 a month. In effect, all this scurrying around amounted to a crash course in small-business management. Japp surprised himself once that summer by using the phrase "pro forma" in a conversation, without thinking twice about it. In August they incorporated as Porta-Flex Products Ltd. And in early September they received their loan from the ODC — $35,000 at 9½ percent interest, with no principal payments for the first nine months.

The terms could scarcely be described as soft-hearted. At that point in time, 9½ percent would have been a fairly steep rate for a commercial loan from a private bank. The ODC, since its inception, had loaned more than $35 million, and more than half of this sum went to foreign-controlled companies. Many of these loans were forgivable — in effect, outright gifts to some very large companies. As Japp concedes, the ODC was co-operative and helpful. But in its handling of the Porta-Flex loan, the ODC didn't leave itself open to charges of excessive generosity.

The next step was two months of hard physical work. The five partners, along with a few ex-Dunlop employees who pitched in for old times' sake — and perhaps the prospect of a job later on — worked 12-hour days, without pay, getting the new plant ready for operation. They had to tear down one large concrete-block wall, hammer an office area together, sweep out and cart away several tons of accumulated junk. Finally, with the help of a 35-ton crane, they moved the handrail press, a piece of machinery as large as a single-car garage, into its new premises, and spent two weeks of 14-hour days tinkering with its steam pipes and electrical connections. "It was one or two in the morning before we got everything connected," Japp recalls. "So then we pressed the button. The machine gave a shudder and a roar — remember, it hadn't been used for six months — and then everything slipped into place and it ran smoothly. Gee, it was beautiful. This was a dead thing, and we'd brought it back to life."

The handrail press ran smoothly, and so, relatively speaking, did the company. The partners' assessment of the handrail market turned out to be conservative. Porta-Flex received its first order from the Toronto Transit Commission, worth several thousand dollars, even before the press was installed. By the time the plant began operating on November 27, 1970, there was already a work backlog of several weeks. By the following January, the plant went to two shifts a day to handle the demand and, the following April, to three shifts a day. Before the end of 1971, Porta-Flex was operating 24 hours a day, seven days a week, and employed 13 people, most of them ex-Dunlop employees, plus the five founders.

Walter Merkel was president, but he was the only partner who could remotely be described as an executive. Japp, Fisher, Cross and Halliday worked on the factory floor, just as they'd always done. Merkel handled sales, which turned out to be largely a matter of informing certain key customers of Porta-Flex's existence, until he left the company the following June. Then Japp doubled as plant manager and as company front man, traveling to such exotic locales as Ottawa and Omaha in search of tariff protection and foreign orders. Porta-Flex even received enquiries from Sao Paulo, Brazil, where a new subway system was being built.

It was funny: the plant looked roughly like what the men had been accustomed to all their working lives: the same machines, the same layout, the same operations with the same materials. But it *felt* utterly different, because they were working for themselves, not somebody else. "This is our company now," Japp told one visitor soon after the plant opened, "so we're awfully cost-conscious. It's a lot different from the old days on Queen Street. There, it didn't seem to matter so much. Sure, we were concerned about doing a good job. But in a big company, it's hard to get personally involved.

"I'll tell you one phrase you used to hear a lot around Queen Street: 'That's good enough.' You don't hear that phrase around here. Every foot of handrail that goes out of this place has our personal stamp on it. Your reputation is riding on it, so it better be good."

This sense of personal involvement showed in small ways. After a man left the washroom, he turned off the light — after all, it was his hydro bill. When the sun shone through the big window on one side of the room, someone usually turned down the thermostat. Cliff Yates, one of the ex-Dunlop men they hired, had spent most of his working life on Queen Street. On his first week in his new job, Yates noticed that the handrails, once the various layers of fabric and rubber had been assembled, were held in shape by a series of clamps, before being fed into the vulcanizing press. So, without saying much about it, and on his own time, he hammered together a long metal trough that did the same job more effectively. A small feat of ingenuity, perhaps. But in all his years at Dunlop, Yates had simply done what he was told — mainly because no one had ever asked him for his own ideas on how to do his job.

The first year at Porta-Flex was a fat one. The company earned $40,000 after taxes, and that was *after* each of the five partners took a $6,000 bonus, in addition to their salaries of between $10,000 and $12,000, to cover the months they'd worked without pay. At Dunlop, Japp had never earned more than $7,500 a year. In his first year as a capitalist, he earned about $18,000.

But already he was restless. His partners were happy with the way the firm was going, but Japp felt the need for another challenge. "The initial setting-up and the struggle was all done. I wasn't ready to settle down in another goddam niche. If I learned anything at Dunlop, it was this: I'll never stick around again unless I'm perfectly satisfied. That doesn't mean you quit at the first sign of an obstacle — but it means you keep trying to do what you want."

By this time, Japp was inhabiting a vastly different world. When it was necessary, he lunched at restaurants that would have been alien territory a year before. He spent more time wearing a suit. He kept most of his old friends, but made a lot of new ones. He grew a moustache. At the age of 44, he became a grandfather; but he actually looked younger than he had the previous year.

His material lifestyle hadn't changed much. Japp has a strong thrifty streak. His family's tiny house is paid for, and he hasn't owned a car for 10 years. He banked most of his extra salary and, in most outward respects, lived about the same as he always had. The old itch for possessions that he'd felt as a youngster was gone now. "When I was young," he explained, "I wanted one of everything in the Eaton's catalogue. But now, what do I need? I've got my house; I've got four suits; I've got my health; I've got well-adjusted offspring."

Everything felt different now. His mind was busy — not with fantasies, but with problems that needed to be solved, decisions that had to be made. He worked hard, but now it didn't seem like work, exactly — but more like an extension of himself. He'd become an entrepreneur — a man who gets his kicks from dreaming up ideas, then trying to make them happen.

And so, in February 1973, he sold his share in Porta-Flex to the three remaining partners and, for $4,000, bought control of Great Eastern Linings, the small company that operated in another part of the building Porta-Flex occupied in Ajax. He ran it for a year, the same way he'd run Porta-Flex: by doing roughly the same sort of things he'd done at Dunlop, but doing them for himself. Early in 1974, one of his customers made him the offer that led to his third venture: the Tip Top Products division that made rubber and vinyl linings for industrial installations. The division, with all its equipment and machinery, had to move. Besides, it was losing money. Would Japp handle the move to a new location, and run the company for $250 a week, on the understanding that he'd own the company if were profitable in two years? "I gamble on people," said Tip Top's owner, "because I can afford to."

Japp accepted. Early in 1974, he had the Great Eastern operation installed in one corner of the old Toronto dairy building, and Tip Top's machinery set up on the rest of the two floors. He'd also persuaded Goodyear to grant him the Canadian distributorship for its dunnage bags, a sort of inflatable rubber bladders that shippers use for padding fragile shipments in boxcars. The things cost from $300 to $800 each, and Japp had worked out a scheme whereby a customer, instead of buying the bag, would lease it from Japp, with the cost of any repairs included in the rental.

Early one morning, on a working day that was to last well past supper time, Japp sat down on a cardboard carton among the rubble that would soon be his office, smoked a cigarette, and talked about how it was 'hen, and how it is now. "You know," he said, "I used to be the most security-conscious bastard who ever put on shoes. Not any more. My whole concept of retirement has changed. At Dunlop, I was starting to look forward to it. Now I can't think of anything worse than having nothing to do. And I'm through planning for 1980. I can make my own security as I go along.

"How does it feel? Well, it's a feeling of freedom. It's hard to say this without sounding trite and phony, but I have the feeling of being in control of my own destiny. If you foul up, you have nobody to blame but yourself.

"It's a way of life. Only it's a way of life where you have more control and direction than you did before. A lot more problems to solve. The truth is, everybody's not cut out for it. I guess I am. But I'd never have known that if they hadn't shut down Dunlop."

5

WILSON SOUTHAM: TOWARD THE MAOIST CORPORATION

The film had been shot at two frames per second, with the camera mounted in the ceiling of a dentist's office. So what you saw, in the screening room of a company called Cox Systems Ltd., was an overhead view of a dentist and his assistant filling a patient's tooth, a job that usually takes 10 or 15 minutes. But at two frames per second, the film compressed this action to about a minute of furious, comical activity, like an old Keystone Cops chase sequence. The dentist's hands flicked in and out of the patient's mouth, faster than a snake's tongue. The assistant flipped back and forth between the chair and a nearby cabinet, so often and so fast that her movements reminded you of the piston on a toy steam engine. The dentist was almost a blur too — reaching out, seizing instruments, twisting his neck around to peer inside the patient's mouth, dashing off-camera to get something, reappearing a split-second later with a new instrument in his hand, and then . . . CUT TO:

Same overhead view; another dentist in another office. This time, the dentist is seated on a stool, but his assistant is zipping in and out of the frame like a mechanical shuttle. At other times she stands beside him, watching his speeded-up hands fluttering at the patient's mouth, strangely motionless in this hyperactive tableau. Larry Levin, a young dentist who is a consultant to Cox Systems, was the cameraman on this 10-minute movie, which is becoming an underground classic among dentists. He is screening the film for me, and provides his own voice-over commentary.

"Now, here's another guy working with sit-down equipment. A recent graduate — *look at that posture!*" At this point, the movie dentist, still in his seated position, is corkscrewing his torso around for a clearer view of the mouth. The poor bastard looks as though he's trying to crawl through a second-story window.

"Look at him moving around," cries Dr. Levin, as the movie dentist squirms and flutters. But then the dentist becomes motionless for several seconds. But there are occasional jerky motions; he is waiting for something, he is fidgeting, he looks unhappy.

"Now he's waiting for the anesthetic," says Levin.

The assistant dashes in and out.

"Look at her," says Levin. "Look how much *assisting* she does, and see if it looks like she's participating." No, she isn't; the dentist's hands are fluttering again, but she's shut out of the action. "She just *sits* there," says Levin ". . . puts in a suction . . . and then she goes and gets something. She shouldn't really have to go anywhere, but she keeps running around."

The film keeps switching from one dentist to another: fat dentists, skinny dentists, bald dentists, hairy ones. But as the film progresses, you notice something else. Each one is working more smoothly than the last. By the final sequence, which shows a Hamilton dentist named Don Coburn, there is hardly any motion at all. Neither Dr. Coburn nor his assistant leave their stools. She grabs instruments from a tray positioned behind the patient's head, and hands them to Coburn when he needs them. Even to a layman, it looks almost beautiful. The motion flows, the hands flutter like hummingbirds, the bodies move scarcely at all. Larry Levin enjoys watching this part, the *denouement* of a film that is helping to revolutionize the practice of dentistry. "Look at her!" he exclaims. "See, now she's getting the filling ready for it . . . *here it comes*! Look . . . she's starting to squirt it in. He didn't have that fidgeting two- or three-minute break."

The film ends and the screen goes white. Levin leans back in his chair, looking pleased. He's seen this film dozens of times, but it always entertains him, makes him feel good.

Cox Systems Ltd. is a small manufacturing company with a

plant at Stoney Creek, Ontario, near Hamilton. You could say that its business is making dental equipment — shiny cabinets with doors and buttons and drawers and a tray that swings out on the end of an anodized aluminum arm. The object itself looks prosaic, not much different from those modular units for storing books and the hi-fi that you see in Danish furniture stores. But to say that Cox Systems makes cabinetry for dentists is like saying the IBM makes adding machines. Truly, Cox may be one of the more unusual companies in North America — not only because of what it makes and how it markets it, but also because of the way the company has tried to organize itself to do these things. In a continent where most large corporations are structured like Stalinist dictatorships, Cox Systems has deliberately tried to behave like a democracy, with power shared between everybody who works there, and decisions arrived at by a consensus process that sometimes resembles group therapy. In this company, the secretaries (who are called information co-ordinators) vote on whether or not the president (whom everybody calls by his first name) will get a raise next year. The president punches a time clock along with everybody else; and the decision to install one was arrived at only after a long and painful process of achieving consensus. What they're really trying to do at Cox is to create a new kind of corporate entity, run along lines that can only be described as Maoist.

The object isn't to maximize profit (although it is conceded that a decent amount of profit is necessary to ensure the company's survival); nor is the object necessarily to grow. If the company remained forever at its 1974 sales volume of about $2 million, that would be fine with Cox, so long as its *real* objective is being met: to provide good lives for Cox's 50-odd employees by showing dentists how to liberate themselves from drudgery. The whole thing is an experiment in communications, both within the company and outside it. And in this context, the cabinetry the company manufactures is almost an incidental by-product. So, for that matter, are profits.

Corporate Maoism can lead to some novel manifestations of inter-office behavior. Here, for instance, is the text of a memo that Cox's president, Wilson Southam, circulated to about half the firm's employees after one of their number quit the company to take a government job. We'll call the employee Margaret.

"During the conversation [in which she told Southam she was quitting] it was clear that Marg has been suffering a really cruel amount of stress, while doing nothing to load any of the rest of us with her problems. The points which Marg made were: The profane and explicit sexual language I use bothers her very, very much. She felt that I was using it deliberately, and she felt that I knew exactly how much it bothered her. She felt also that I was and had been getting at her with a variety of remarks made over a long period of time. She found the constant urging to head for the next target exhausting, and suggested that this might be a negative motivator for others in the group. She asked if there would never be a plateau, a time for dialogue.

"Now, if everyone who had ever left a group had had the guts and intelligence to frame points and questions of this explicit quality and then put them, there would be one hell of a lot fewer problems between people.

"Pretty clearly, all of what Marg said calls for serious consideration, and more than likely some serious behavior change on my part. So that's what it's going to get. And any insight any of you can offer as individuals will be appreciated.

"Meanwhile, as I sit glimpsing the corner of a really lovely vegetable garden, a hanging flower pot bursting with blooms and a thickly tangled section of country woods, I know that I will miss Marg, regret my part in her decision to go and am profoundly grateful she has chosen to be so thoughtfully honest."

What kind of management style is this? Why is Wilson Southam laying this embarrassing piece of self-accusation on his employees? Why, for that matter, is he telling them about his vegetable garden? Southam's memos to the people at Cox are probably unique in the annals of inter-office correspondence. One week, he may favor them with a 10-page memo that intricately describes his day from the time he got up ("6:30 Phone rings in room at Gulliver's Motel . . . stumble up feeling drained . . . up, wash, to hell with shaving . . .") to the time he left the office ("5:45: Resolve to take the rest of the evening off as I am rapidly becoming useless to others. Good night."). Another time, it may be an elaborate exhortation for everybody to work like hell for the next 10 weeks to get the new product line out to customers, because if they don't the company may have a serious cash-flow problem. He calls this 10-week period Operation Keep-the-Restaurant-Open.

Another memo may be a rambling discourse on the nature of freedom and responsibility, or a discussion of the new floor layout in the manufacturing section of the plant. Or it may be a wounded dissertation on the fact that some money has been filched from a wallet, a projector is missing, and $5 has been taken from a desk drawer: "The cost is not the dollars lost. The cost is the erosion of HIGH TRUST AND LOW FEAR. The whole thing is very sad."

Sometimes Southam sounds like a camp counsellor, sometimes like a sociologist. Sometimes he sounds like the leader of a group-therapy session. Sometimes he sounds like Marshall McLuhan. What he never sounds like is the president of a $2-million corporation, for Wilson Southam is an extraordinary sort of entrepreneur. What interests him most isn't the products that Cox Systems develops and builds and sells; it's the process by which these things are accomplished, and what happens to the lives of the people who build and sell them and the people who buy and use them. He has an elegant Oxford education, an independent income, a background in muckraking television journalism, and a dream that has possessed certain visionary factory owners (Engels, Lord Shaftesbury, John Stewart Mill) since the dawn of the industrial revolution: to use the corporation as the vehicle for creating new and better kinds of human relationships.

Southam's family, an extended clan whose members have been active for several generations in publishing, diplomacy and various forms of cultural uplift, is about as close as you can get in this country to a native aristocracy. The family still controls what the Senate Report on the Mass Media called "the oldest, largest and most diversified media group in Canada" — with interests in a string of daily newspapers whose total circulation is close to a million; in the weekly Financial Times of Canada; in more than 40 industrial and professional periodicals; and in a few radio stations. Being a Southam in Canada isn't quite like being a Cecil in England. But it's very much like being a Molson, or an Eaton, or a Timmins, or a Gooderham: you possess a name that is recognized and deferred to anywhere in the country. You are a member of a commercial dynasty whose name has been imprinted on the consciousness of the millions of people who buy its products; and it is difficult to get people to treat you as anything less than somewhat special.

Wilson Southam managed to escape the dangers of being a Southam by growing up mostly in the west, where his father was advertising manager and later publisher of the Southam-owned Calgary Herald. He spent seven years prepping at the exclusive Trinity College School in Port Hope, Ontario, then returned to Calgary, "where nobody gives a damn if you're a Southam or not." There was something anti-elitist in his nature from the start. From the time he was 13, he was hitch-hiking all over North America. He worked as a cowboy and as a licensed pony-boy in the Rockies. He drove a motorcycle from El Salvador to Canada. He became one of the continent's better skiers (at 17, he placed fourth in the combined slalom and downhill event in the North American championships). His real education came from mountains, and from all kinds of people he rubbed against through an adventurous adolescence. By the time he entered McGill University in 1953, his main academic interest was philosophy. It was a passion that sent him to the head of his freshman class at McGill and, after he'd graduated in 1957, to Balliol College, Oxford, for more philosophy. "When I was studying philosophy," Southam recalls, "I thought myself to the point of insanity. I just let go — I went right into the solipsistic thing, I went into the nonsense of language, I went into the empiricists and rationalists, right through to Kant.

"What philosophy did was to lift me out of what culture had already done to me. Today, I don't think I do anything just because I feel I ought to. I do things today because I see in my head some sort of relevance, some sort of meaningfulness in doing it. Not a hell of a lot, but better than none."

You might almost say that philosophy liberated him. Most of us tend to drift through life, buffeted by currents of fear, of habit, of upbringing, of chance — forces that we perceive only dimly. But Southam, by his early 20s, had acquired the knack of living purposefully — of deciding what he did and didn't want, and acting in accordance with those decisions. I don't mean he's obsessively ambitious, a man driven by a single goal. But I think he's more conscious than most people of what he's doing and why he's doing it. There is something *focused* about him. Whether conferring with a group of designers, or eating a salad, or executing a tricky dive into the pool on the grounds of his home outside Ottawa, Southam always seems to be *right there*, fully inhabiting the moment. It's partly a matter of concentration, but there's something else: a clarity, an intensity that you find only in people who know exactly who they are. Philosophy helped Southam get there. But so, I suspect, did the fact that, for several years in his late adolescence, he thought he was going to die. A kidney ailment he contracted when he was 17 was diagnosed as a terminal condition. As it turned out, the doctors were wrong. But the prospect of an early death made him serious in the best sense: he learned not to waste his time or talents or energy.

When he returned to Canada from Oxford in 1959, Southam had a new wife named Beverley and at least two clear notions about what he wanted to do with his life. His work would involve communications, and it would involve human behavior. This was an extension of Southam's philosophical pursuits, and you could sum it up in a maxim he still uses today: "Information is freedom." Like a number of other thinkers, Southam had begun to view society in terms of information-flows; streams of data that determine who we are and how we live and how we perceive the world. And he could see that the advent of mass markets and mass media was changing the ways in which power can be exercised.

A century earlier, the dean of Balliol, the fabled Benjamin Jowett, had been a dominant presence not only in his college but in the intellectual life of Victorian England. An undergraduate had written of him:

I am the master of this college,
What I don't know isn't knowledge.

That satirical couplet told more than it intended. For Jowett, with his wit and his classical erudition, perfectly exemplified an age when knowledge was the monopoly of a cultivated few. And it was this information monopoly that enabled the inhabitants of a small island to govern half the earth.

Southam inherited this elite tradition, but could see that it was ending. "I always felt comfortable with people of all sorts of back-

80

grounds," he explains, "and I began very early to recognize that it's the literate, abstract background — the *verbal* background — that leads to power in our society. But I also saw that it was going to do so less and less. Look at what a plumber earns today; he doesn't have to be articulate at all. The whole thing of mass markets has had a tremendous equalizing effect. It's redistributed power away from the verbal people. Today, everybody has power." Although Southam may not have articulated it in quite this way, he came back from Balliol with a sort of a mission: he wanted to help people use this new power, the power of freely available information, to improve their lives.

And so he took up journalism, which is not a hard trade to break into if your name is Southam. He spent six intensive months setting up a series of trusts that guaranteed him and his young family a comfortable and virtually inexhaustible income; then spent three years as a reporter on the Southam-owned Hamilton Spectator. He spent some of his spare time and energy researching with a Hamilton dentist named Don Coburn — of whom we have heard and will hear more — the feasibility of building a ski hill on Hamilton Mountain. (The parks board accepted their recommendation, and the hill is still in use.)

In 1963, Southam left The Spectator to join the Canadian Broadcasting Corp.'s public affairs department in Ottawa as a TV producer. He lasted only three years in television. But in that time he produced a phenomenal 65 programs, helped create the most exciting public-affairs programming the CBC ever broadcast before or since and from CBC top management's point of view became one of the most troublesome employees they'd ever hired. Southam was one of a small coterie of producers — Douglas Leiterman, Patrick Watson, Ross McLean and Beryl Fox were others — who helped to revolutionize television journalism in the early 1960s by fully exploiting the medium's visual potential instead of treating TV as an extension of print, or as "illustrated radio." They also adapted freely from the techniques of tabloid journalism: hidden cameras; interviews so carefully staged they often became exercises in psychodrama; investigative reporting; satire.

Southam started out on an Ottawa program called Enquiry, then produced by Patrick Watson. But he also helped plan the format of an hour-long Sunday night program which, in three stormy seasons, generated more controversy and attracted a larger audience than any public-affairs show in the CBC's history: This Hour Has Seven Days. When Seven Days was at the peak of its popularity in 1965, its impact was unbelievable. Every Monday morning, newspapers routinely carried follow-up stories to revelations that had been aired the night before on Seven Days. In some towns, most activity simply stopped at 10 o'clock on Sunday night. Dinner parties adjourned to the TV set; families skipped bowling. Maclean's magazine discovered that in one small Ontario town the local waterworks experienced a sharp upsurge in demand at precisely those times between 10 and 11 p.m. when Seven Days paused for station breaks. Most of the town, apparently, waited for those pauses before walking from the TV set to the bathroom.

Much of this success was rooted in Southam's notions of how information should be shared. "In those days," he says, "there was a tendency for TV producers to program for people by whom they wanted to be intellectually accepted. *We* felt our responsibility was to program at the level of awareness and comprehension of the kind of people we'd probably never meet — the mass TV audience. We tried to get inside their heads, come in at a level where they could buy it, understand it, follow it — and stop at the point where they were starting to get bored."

This usually meant using a magazine format: a lively succession of short items, with heavy themes carefully balanced by funny ones. It sometimes involved carefully "building" an issue, a technique that Southam used several times on a local information show called 7½ Citizens, with devastating effect. "You can't generate mass interest with a single item," Southam explains. "Watergate is a good example. But if you keep coming back to it week after week, and if the subject is right, you can slowly build it into a matter of major concern. We'd start an issue and nobody would be interested. We'd use satire to get their interest, or any other technique that seemed to work. And by the time we'd built the subject up to a half-hour program, we had a sort of city-wide hysteria going. The strategy was one of building involvement — short attention spans, the widest possible variety of techniques, lots of irreverence."

The irreverence, more than anything, may have been what

killed Seven Days. The CBC is a large and cautious bureaucracy, and its relationships with the Ottawa legislators who provide its funds are always delicate. Seven Days, Enquiry and 7½ Citizens exposed and ridiculed politicians regularly. What was worse, in doing so they frequently disobeyed management directives. Once, when British Prime Minister Harold Wilson gave a news conference in Ottawa, the CBC's management decreed that it should not be shown on Seven Days, since this was a "news" item not a "public affairs" item, and thus the responsibility of another department. Southam ignored the order, borrowed film of the conference from a private Ottawa station and aired it that Sunday on Seven Days. By its third season, there were fears within the CBC's headquarters that Watson and Leiterman, the co-producers of Seven Days, were becoming political powers in their own right. Southam and his boss, Bernard Ostry, who constituted the Seven Days presence in Ottawa, knew more people and had more influence than many CBC administrators. "There was a long-standing attempt to get us out of Ottawa." Southam recalls. "The people in head office were paranoid in their belief that we were talking to the MPs and causing them problems in Parliament. They didn't want an Ottawa unit with any articulate, thoughtful people in it."

The final crunch came over a Southam-produced series called The Public Eye. He'd broadcast several satirical items (including one memorable sequence where he'd flown Larry Zolf to London, to auction off seats in the Canadian Senate at Speaker's Corner in Hyde Park). The worst flak, however, came after a Public Eye crew had shot a sequence inside the halls of Parliament. There were wild rumors that Southam's crew had bribed Parliamentary security guards with booze, to the point where some were falling-down drunk. ("They weren't drunk," says Southam. "They'd been knocked out by the fumes of the E. B. Eddy paper mill across the river.")

Southam found himself one afternoon in the office of a CBC vice-president, being chewed out for his various transgressions. "And while I sat there listening to this stream of abuse," Southam recalls, "I thought, 'You know, Wilson, between Enquiry and 7½ Citizens you've really taken the shots you want to take. From here on in, you'll have that old journalistic problem: you'll be looking for stories, or manufacturing concern, some of the time at least. You won't have that nice feeling in your guts that each program you're doing is something you really give a shit about.' " And so, against the urgings of his friends, he resigned.

Later, when the CBC cancelled Seven Days after its third season, the matter was deemed to be of sufficient political importance to justify a Parliamentary inquiry. As a result of its findings, Southam and Ross McLean (the victim of a separate CBC purge) were reinstated. That same day Southam resigned again, his point made. He'd worked his way through journalism, creating one hell of a fuss in the process, and learned several crucial lessons about the nature of large organizations, and what motivates the people who work for them.

One of his last CBC assignments had been a 13-part documentary series on Queen's University. It was one of those assignments that seemed hopeless from the start. Management had denied the project the overtime that Southam felt it required, and he was working with technicians who were accustomed to filing grievances at the drop of a microphone cable. So he did something that is almost unprecedented in the annals of the CBC: he called the technicians together and asked them how *they* would like the programs to be. He invited them to participate in a collective production, and they responded. In seven weeks of shooting, Southam never slept more than four hours a night. The crew worked just as hard, and even contributed 25 hours of overtime, which included staging a final party, where they asked Southam to make a speech. "I talked for about 45 minutes about what people out there weren't getting on the box. What our responsibilities were. About the bureaucracy, and other problems that beset us. I tore hell out of the CBC. I'm told they still show the videotape of that speech to this day, although management's never seen it."

When the crew returned to Ottawa, the technicians didn't file grievances over all the jurisdictional corners that had been cut to complete the programs. Not only that, but they actually sent a delegation to management, armed with figures showing that by working as a team in Kingston they'd produced their programs at about one-third the cost the corporation anticipated, even with overtime premiums included. "And they'd done it," says Southam, "by running, by caring, by having better ideas for the shots, by helping performers, by doing all the things that are latent in those crews that don't get a chance to emerge very often. They did it by being allowed to utilize their full professionalism."

For Southam, the lesson was clear. Many huge organizations — not just the CBC — provide working environments that are deeply unsatisfying for most lower-echelon employees — not just because they're treated like interchangeable parts in a large and unwieldy machine, forced into narrow occupational roles that deprive their jobs of real meaning. These people have the knowledge to perform skilled technical jobs; but most organizations treat them as though they had no power, no judgment, no knowledge, no right to perceive the overall picture.

In the fall of 1966, about the time he was busy quitting the CBC, Southam had invested $75,000 in a small company started by Don Coburn, the Hamilton dentist with whom he'd worked on the ski hill project. The company was called Cox Dental Manufacturing Co. Ltd. It consisted almost entirely of Dr. Coburn, who'd designed a chairside dentist's cabinet in his spare time, and Ron Cox, a local machinist and tool-maker who with one or two helpers built the units one at a time in a cluttered workshop a few doors away from Coburn's office.

Dr. Coburn had graduated from the University of Toronto's School of Dentistry in 1951, practised for a few years in Ancaster, Ontario, then moved to Hamilton "where I could take fewer patients, and take the time to learn dentistry properly." He was an innovator by nature and, in his new office, he set aside a separate operating room that contained the experimental devices he'd begun to develop. He was tinkering on the most basic level. One month he might try overhead lighting, instead of the swivel-mounted lamp that most dentists use. Another month, it might be a mobile cuspidor — the little metal bowl that patients spit into, but mounted on a swivel arm, instead of attached to the arm of the traditional dental unit. He'd even taken out a few patents, notably for a device called Vacu-Matic, a funnel-shaped cup connected to a vacuum tube, which replaced the traditional cuspidor.

By the early 1960s, Coburn had become a recognized expert in one of the most neglected areas of dentistry: the whole question of the comfort and efficiency of the dentist. His interest was perhaps spurred by the fact that he had varicose veins, and was forced to sit down at his work. Today, sit down dentistry is common and will soon become the norm. In 1960, when Coburn started having trouble with his legs, there were fewer than a dozen dentists in the whole country who worked that way.

Technological advance is what made sit-down dentistry possible. Reclining chairs came on the market in the 1950s. So did high-speed drills, which required large volumes of water flowing into the patient's mouth to keep the tooth cool. And so did high-volume suction pumps, which could drain away all that water.

What Coburn realized — and what few equipment manufacturers even today have realized — is that sit-down dentistry makes possible a whole new system of physical and spatial relationships. Every element in the operating environment — the assistant, the equipment, the trays that hold the instruments, everything — can be orchestrated into a unity of time and motion that can make a dentist far more productive and leave him feeling fresh at the end of a day.

"Most dentists are pretty wiped at the end of a day," says Larry Levin, the young dentist who worked on Dr. Coburn's time-and-motion film and is now a consultant to Cox. "There's a lot of physical stress in doing the job. It's tiring to do something repetitively. And if you're uncomfortable physically, as well as suffering from the psychological fatigue that comes from doing the same thing over and over, you're doubly wiped." Dr. Levin finds it not in the least surprising that dentists have one of the highest suicide and divorce rates of any occupational group.

Coburn's most dramatic innovation, although it didn't look in the least dramatic, was the system he first developed between 1964 and 1966, with design assistance from David Jenkins, one of his patients who was then a student at the Ontario College of Art. It was called a Chairside System, a free-standing cabinet designed to be positioned behind the patient's chair. The side facing the dentist contained shelves and cupboards. On the other side was a working space for the dental assistant. In between was a small darkroom for developing X-rays. It doesn't sound terribly innovative; but, says Coburn, "everybody got excited. I used a unit in my lecture demonstrations at the University of Toronto, and seven or eight students wanted to buy one after they graduated. One dentist in Chicago wanted six units. All of a sudden we had $60,000 worth of orders, and we didn't have the capacity to fill them."

What made the Chairside System so special? One clear innovation was the louvres in the cabinet's face, through which the hoses and cables for the various instruments were fed. It seems almost *too* simple, but this was an important improvement on the rather complicated retraction devices then in use in most dentists' offices. But the crucial innovation — again, it sounds absurdly simple — was Coburn's approach to traffic flow. In the Coburn system, the dentist and his assistant sat on opposite sides of the patient's chair. And when they got up to fetch something, their paths were on opposite sides of the chairside unit.

That was the beginning of Cox Dental Manufacturing Co. Ltd. "I didn't want to go into business full-time," says Dr. Coburn, "but Ron Cox said he wouldn't do the work unless I gave him half the business. He used his leverage when he had it, and I don't blame him. It was totally fair as far as I was concerned. Ron was putting his blood and guts into the thing."

Ron Cox worked all that winter with two assistants in a third-floor workshop on Hamilton's Haymarket Street, just around the corner from Coburn's office. In the spring, they delivered 16 units at $1,600 apiece. That was when Coburn approached Wilson Southam for additional funds. He wanted to keep Cox's three employees on the payroll through the year, building components for more Chairside Systems. Southam made the investment, which gave him a one-third interest in Cox, through one of the venture companies he'd set up at the beginning of his journalistic career. He stayed regularly in touch by phone from Ottawa, where he'd taken a part-time teaching post at Carleton University.

By the spring of 1967, it was apparent that something was wrong. After the initial flurry of orders, Cox Manufacturing didn't sell another unit. Southam decided to get more fully involved. "I was on the phone to them all the time anyway, so I started going down to Hamilton more and more. First two days a week. Then three. By mid-1967 it was a full-time job." He still works five days a week in Hamilton, and spends weekends at home in Ottawa with his family.

For people who didn't know Southam well, it seemed like a weird decision. Why would a scion of one of Canada's first families, a gifted and independently wealthy TV producer, want to commute to *Hamilton*, for God's sake, to sell cupboards to dentists? "Quite a few good friends thought I'd lost my mind. It wasn't respectable, compared to being a TV producer. It wasn't as much fun. It wasn't as bright."

Southam, of course, knew exactly what he was doing and why. In television, he'd been trying to use communication to change behavior. He'd even spent a great deal of the CBC's money on surveys aimed at discovering whether the programs he produced effected any measurable change in public attitudes. The short answer is that they didn't.

But as he learned about the dental industry and about dentists generally and about the lamentable state of North American teeth, he began to realize that Cox could provide him with the platform that journalism had failed to deliver. The way to build the company, he decided, was not by selling cupboards to dentists; but by re-educating dentists into adopting behavior patterns that would mean working less, earning more and delivering better service to the public at less cost. Marshall McLuhan once observed that IBM didn't start to grow until it realized it wasn't selling adding machines; it was in the data-processing business. Southam embraced the same approach: Develop software systems, (re-educating dentists) and hardware (the Chairside System that Dr. Coburn had developed) as part of a single package.

At this point, the subject of all this theorizing consisted of an insolvent five-man organization with no assets, no sales and no prospects, housed in a third-floor, walk-up workshop. Southam set about building the company from scratch. He renamed it Cox Systems — not, he insists, because "systems" was just then a fashionable word; but because he really did want to develop systems, not just hardware. His early hiring decisions were crucial. For sales, he hired Doug Young, a young MBA who'd held junior executive jobs with Stelco and the Canadian Imperial Bank of Commerce. As bookkeeper, he hired Shirley Ritchie, who later became corporate secretary and a key member of the Cox team. As designer, he hired David Jenkins, who'd helped Dr. Coburn design the Chairside System while he was still attending the Ontario College of Art. About a year later Southam and Coburn bought out Ron Cox's one-third interest in the company; Cox's style didn't mesh with kind of company Southam was trying to create.

With the nucleus of a team assembled, Southam set about putting his hardware-software theories into practice. By the end of 1968, the thing was starting to come together. The team had developed a full line of products and, more important, had refined the systems to go with thm. For once, the word "systems" wasn't being used to impress the stock market, because the Cox team really had developed a system. There was a kind of seamless unity about the products themselves and the way these products were introduced to dentists.

The products consisted of variations on Don Coburn's original theme. The unit that incorporated an X-ray darkroom was discontinued (the market wasn't strong enough). In its place, the Cox team developed four separate modules, each designed to play a specific role in a dentist's office: a chairside system and a chairside lab, a storage lab and an assistant's unit. They all look simple, but they're immensely sophisticated; not so much in the way they're made — although some units have as many as 500 non-cabinetry parts — but in the way they're designed to be used. Their modules are actually tools that, when used in the correct interface with a dentist and his assistant, permit interruption-free dentistry. The major units range in price from $3,200 to $5,000 each.

Cox has a continent-wide network of dealers, and does not sell direct to dentists. But the company communicates its ideas to them in an environment that is relentlessly educational. There are two formats for this process: the clinics, which are arranged by dealers for local dentists, at which Cox people outline their approach to dentistry; and the seminars, held at Cox's headquarters in Stoney Creek. The clinics, including a coffee break, last an evening. The seminars take a whole working day, and are limited to about 10 dentists at a time, plus whatever staff they choose to bring along. The company also has a facility-planning department, which creates office plans and interior designs as part of the overall package. What they're selling is a process, not a product;

and the process is aimed at the total re-education of dentists and their staffs. No, the seminars aren't thinly disguised sales pitches; the dentists who attend them pay their own way, and fly to Stoney Creek from all over the continent. Cox personnel seem to be regarded by dentists not as salesmen, but almost as management consultants. And the seminars, through professional word-of-mouth, have acquired a considerable underground reputation.

Much of the seminars' content is about operating efficiency — traffic flows, the role of assistants, and the number of interruptions a dentist must face while working on a patient's mouth. Thus, the Coburn fast-motion film, which was made in 1968 with the aid of a grant from the Design Branch of the federal Department of Industry, Trade and Commerce, is always shown. Every dentist who sees it recognizes his own working habits. For some, watching the film can be a profoundly disturbing experience. "It is," says one Cox employee, "the beginning of enlightenment."

For some dentists, the seminars also change the way they think about their assistants. "The traditional way of looking at it," says Larry Levin, "is that you do everything yourself. The 'anointed hand' is a concept you learn in dental school. You're the only one who can do it, and everybody else is peripheral. In fact, it's just the opposite. In a modern office, the whole thing will collapse if any member of the team isn't there. I sometimes think that more activity can go on if the dentist *isn't* there. But if your assistant's gone, you don't even know where things are kept in the lab."

But the crux of the Cox system isn't the "how" of dentistry, but the "why". Most dentists, the Cox people believe, are as bored as workers on an automotive assembly line, although they're vastly better paid. The main reason dentists are bored, they argue, is the same reason why so many workers are discontented: their work seems repetitive, meaningless and unrewarding. "You come out of dentistry school," says Levin, "and, sure, you feel enthusiastic. You can stay enthusiastic for a while. But at what point do you start feeling tired of doing fillings? The hundredth filling? The two thousandth filling? The *three* thousandth? How many years can you go on, doing yet another silver filling, before you're ready to jump out the window?"

The best answer to this problem, according to the Cox theology, is not to do fillings. The main role of dentistry, in other words, should be disease prevention and health education, not treatment. This notion, more than anything, is the basis of everything Wilson Southam is trying to achieve.

"Dentistry is a monopoly," says Southam, "in the sense that the supply of dentists is inelastic and the demand is elastic as hell. It typifies most of what's worst about professional rip-offs. Dentistry is on the wrong track, in that it waits for you to get sick, and then works on you and makes a lot of money, then waits for you to get sick again. But we now know that dental disease is totally preventable. Nobody should ever have to have a filling. With the right diet and the right care, cavities won't happen. Considering what's now known about positive health, merely to treat the disease is gross irresponsibility." Neither of his two kids, Southam is fond of reminding people, have ever had a cavity.

The company's mission, then, is nothing less than to re-orient the profession away from treatment, and in the direction of disease prevention and total health education. The dentist's office, Southam believes, is an ideal unit for this kind of change to occur. "The office is the point where the public meets the health professional. They're still small enough for behavior changes to occur, and they're situated where people can reach them. They tend to have paramedical people on staff, which lowers your unit cost for the delivery of information. And the fact that dentistry itself has got a solution to dental disease — it all makes the dentist's office a very attractive place for learning how to resource the public with places where they can find out how to enjoy much higher levels of health."

To underline this concern, Southam encouraged Cox's design team to develop a series of modules designed to help dental hygienists teach patients how to care for their teeth. The main unit consists of a counter at which the patient sits; in front of him are eight large transparencies — huge blowups of diseased and healthy teeth. By pushing buttons, the patient or hygienist can illuminate each transparency in turn. The Cox Health Learning System costs $3,500, and it looks like something that was designed for Expo 67. It hasn't sold very well, perhaps because many dentists have concluded that they don't need a costly machine to help them tell patients to brush regularly.

What dentists do seem to appreciate, though, is that the Cox approach enables them to work less stressfully — and make more money. Southam cites the case of one young dentist who, after undergoing the Cox treatment, decided to locate in a small, poverty-stricken village in Eastern Ontario. The town had 2,000 people and two octogenarian dentists. "He came into that town," says Southam, "with a commitment not to do any extractions in the first year, because he didn't want to confuse people. The smart money, the traditional money, really laughed when they heard that he was going to concentrate on preventive dentistry. He hired a receptionist, an assistant and a health-learning co-ordinator who doubles as a hygienist, and nobody's laughing. He grossed $72,000 the first year, and he's doing better than $150,000 a year now."

Southam is passionately intense about communicating with dentists, and the same intensity is also directed inward, toward communicating with Cox's 50-odd employees. The company is housed in a new concrete-block factory building in an industrial subdivision about 10 miles from Hamilton, and one of the first things you notice about the place is that nearly everybody, both in the factory section of the building and in the area devoted to offices, has hung up personal posters somewhere in their working space. Inspirational snippets from Camus, from Fritz Perls and from Snoopy are everywhere. So are copies of a small showcard that enshrines the Four Goals of Cox Systems:

To develop the finest health delivery system company in the world.

To develop our group to support personal satisfaction, "living" and "growing" at work.

To increase autonomy and leverage by using resources wisely.

To contribute to long-term public interest in a "good" way.

That wording was arrived at, like almost every major decision at Cox, after a long, intense and occasionally tiresome process of dialogue, involving a large number of people who, after much soul-searching decided on roughly what Wilson Southam wanted all along.

"Participatory management" has been a corporate buzz word for at least a decade. But few executives have tried so hard to achieve it as has Wilson Southam at Cox Systems. The process has been painful at times. Almost certainly it has been inefficient. Quite possibly it has cost the company several million dollars, in terms of sales it might have made and growth it might have achieved under a more authoritarian structure. But for Southam and for most of Cox's employees, the effort has been worth it. Southam really has distributed power throughout the company, to an extent that amazed at least one outsider. When I approached Southam to begin researching this chapter, he said what corporate presidents very seldom say, and, when they do say it, very seldom mean it: "Go ahead. Cruise around. Find out what's going on. Talk to anybody around here. Don't just take my word for it."

I did cruise around and I did talk to a fair number of Cox people. All of them — and this is what persuaded me that there really is substance to Southam's participatory theories — talked as freely with me as did Southam about the strengths and weaknesses of the company. No one tried to bullshit me. No one seemed afraid. No one was entirely happy with the company, and no one tried to conceal their dissatisfactions. I've interviewed people in police states and I've interviewed people in very large corporations, and the feeling you get in both places is approximately the same. Cox Systems is one of the very few companies of its size I've ever encountered where all the employees, at every echelon, talked and acted like free men and women. Unlike most companies, power really is shared, instead of being concentrated at the top.

Southam: "That's really what we're fooling around with at Cox: the recognition that everybody has power, and that people who aren't educated to that power are in a very dangerous state. The idea that you can pay somebody a salary and hence have authority over them presupposes that they're going to starve if they don't work for you. Well, that's no longer true in today's economy. People, somewhat unconsciously, and at varying rates according to their cultural background, are in effect saying that the old, production-consumption model of classical economics is becoming meaningless to them. They want to live fully, with dignity and all the things that behavioral scientists describe as true motivators — responsibility as *they* perceive it; achievement as *they* perceive it; possibilities for real personal growth, for self-actualization.

"At Cox, this means management's role is primarily as a resource facility — to ensure people get the information, the space, the tools and materials they need to do their jobs properly, and are left alone to do them," Southam says. Most executives deal this way with other executives. But it's unusual to see the principle applied to the factory floor and what used to be called the steno pool.

One Cox designer, for instance, was in the habit of making extremely detailed working drawings. "His whole European training," says Southam, "was to cover those drawings with information — so you could hang anybody who didn't do the thing right. Well, this is all insulting to the guy who builds a cabinet from those drawings, a craftsman who should know what he's doing. If you want a full partnership and a respect for his craftsmanship, you'll give him the critical dimensions — and then let him take care of the variable problems, which he's perfectly competent to do." The designer in question no longer makes such detailed drawings.

People are allowed to make their own mistakes at Cox, and decisions that affect everybody are usually made by everybody. The Great Time Clock Controversy, for instance, arose after the staff voted to work staggered hours. Everyone had to be on the job between the core hours of 10 a.m. and 3 p.m. three days a week; after that they were free to choose when they arrived and left, so long as they worked a full 35-hour week. The controversy arose over whether or not the staggered hours should be policed, and the issue deeply divided the company. Some thought the very idea of a time clock was insulting. Others believed that if it weren't used employees would abuse the staggered-hours privilege. Consensus was finally achieved; a majority wanted the clock, and the minority grudgingly agreed to go along.

The interesting thing is that under the ground rules Southam has developed, anyone could have vetoed that decision, and no time clock would have been installed. "But nobody's ever cast a veto," says Doug Young, the vice-president who, in a conventional company, would be called a sales manager. "From that, you could argue that the system is meaningless and academic. I'd argue from the other side — that it's very meaningful. There was deep-seated dissatisfaction with some of the group decisions. But the people who were dissatisfied believed enough in the group that they accepted that decision, *that* day — knowing that somewhere down the road, on a different day, the decision would go with them, and that both decisions would be in the interests of the group as a whole. So it's a give-and-take process, and it comes from having respect for other people in the group."

Young had a typically frustrating background in large companies. Like several employees I talked to, he felt that working at Cox had changed his head and his life. Even his marriage is participatory. But he doesn't try to oversell the benefits. "The whole experience at Cox isn't peaches and cream," he says. "There's a general consensus about the value of our goals and our structure. But that doesn't mean everybody gets up in the morning with a great big smile on their face and loves every minute of the working day. The thing is fraught with difficulties. There are tremendous interpersonal conflicts. But our structure gives us a better chance to avoid some of those problems. And if they do arise, we've got a better chance to get out of them."

It's foolhardy to speculate whether Cox might have done better or worse under an authoritarian management. As it is, the company's sales grew by 60 percent each year between 1967 and 1972 and it has earned a small profit since 1971, despite heavy expenditures in research and development. The company is unquestionably a leader in its field; the number of Cox innovations that other dental equipment firms have imitated is proof of that. Its staff relations, if the perceptions of an outside observer can be trusted, are uncommonly genial. That's either an adequate performance of an impressive one, depending on how sympathetic you are to the notion of corporate democracy.

The final judgment, as it usually is, will be rendered on the balance sheet. "Sure, we're a Maoist company," says Doug Young. "There are a lot of socialistic aspects to what we're doing. No question. But if we can't make this company profitable, then that's where the socialism thing ends."

Whether or not Cox makes a lot of money, Wilson Southam is satisfied that he's proved his personal point. "Look," he told me. "I could get on a plane with you and travel around North America to city after city, and take you to dentists who would cancel appointments to see us if I phoned on short notice. And they'd sit down and tell you: 'My whole life is different.'

"Well, I couldn't do that after making TV programs, no matter how good the ratings were."

6

THE LUCK OF THE SOUTHERNS — AND HOW ATCO GREW

Don Southern still looks and walks like a fireman. He has a slightly rolling, bandy-legged gait, as though his legs had acquired a permanent curve from spending so many years wrapped around a brass pole. His arms seem to spring outward from his shoulders, instead of hanging straight down, as though they'd been stretched by years of lugging ladders and hoses on and off trucks. No, he does not look remotely like the founder and board chairman of ATCO Industries Ltd., a multi-million-dollar Canadian company; in fact, he would be more plausible as the man who takes your name and license number when you drive past the guardhouse at ATCO's 72-acre industrial park in southwest Calgary.

This industrial park is ATCO's main manufacturing headquarters. It isn't merely a factory. It's a whole *village* of factories, a ferociously busy enclave of large steel buildings and war-surplus sheds. The streets of this village are crawling with fork-lift trucks and big trailer-transports loaded with lumber and steel beams and sheet aluminum. And as you watch him striding through this orgy of wealth and activity that he and his son Ron have created, you can't help wondering what would have happened to Don Southern if his own father hadn't been such a miserable human being.

Southern was 63 when I saw him, still too restless to behave like a semi-retired captain of industry, too tough to be lovable, too much a man of his own past to be a major factor in his company's future.

In one corner of ATCO's industrial park, he has his own little company to play around with — South Park Industries Ltd. It's not part of the ATCO empire, although ATCO has an option to buy South Park when the old man finally retires. He started this little company in 1967, after it became apparent that ATCO had grown too huge and complex and sophisticated to be in urgent need of his talents. His son Ron was running the show utterly, and there wasn't actually a hell of a lot for the old man to do. So he started South Park as a second career, a retirement toy for a man who has too many inner urgencies gnawing at him ever to feel secure, ever to achieve tranquility and repose.

And where did this urgency come from? What was driving this man to build another company of his own, when the one he founded in 1946 was already one of the authentic marvels of Canadian enterprise? I don't know what impels some men to take large risks and work their butts off to start new businesses, while other men are content to live a salaried life. But I do know that one's father must have something to do with it. And Don Southern's father laid burdens on his son that the old man will carry to the grave.

The grandfather emigrated from England in 1913, worked for the Calgary Fire Department until 1929, then founded a gardening business which, by the time he retired, employed nearly 50 people. He was a cold, remote man who worked obsessively, and insisted that everyone around him do the same. But most of the time the Southerns were dirt-poor. The grandfather worked 12-hour shifts at the old number four fire hall, and kept a cow and chickens in the backyard garden. Don Southern, still in knee pants, used to be sent out late at night to steal oats from nearby farms for their animals — and then sent back to pick up the trail of feed that led to the scene of the crime. His first job was hawking the special armistice edition of the Calgary Herald in 1918. When he was 14, Don Southern left home, a departure that did not displease his parent: "My happy father gave me a half a pound of tobacco and a pair of leather gloves. That was the last thing I ever received from him."

Father and son hardly spoke after that. When Don got married at 19 to Ina MacDonald ("actually an elopement without a honeymoon") his father slammed the door in his face when Don came to tell him of the marriage. A year later: "I tried again when

Ronald was born, as I was so proud I was sure this would be the breakthrough. So I phoned to ask if he would like us to bring our son over. The reply was, 'I never want to see any of you.'"

By this time it was the Depression and Don was forced to take successive cuts in his truck driver's pay. He finally quit and went on welfare for $54 a month. "Things were so bad I can remember leaving the house one morning and none of the three of us had anything to eat. I found work cleaning and painting eight lawn-mowers to earn 35 cents. By the end of the day we had bread (four cents a loaf), and hamburger, some butter as well as some eggs."

Everybody's dream of heaven during the Depression was a steady, no-layoff job. When the Calgary Fire Department advertised for 20 men in 1933, several thousand applied. All but 500 were eliminated for being too old, too young, or physically unfit. The rest were subjected to a terrifying series of tests: climbing swaying, 85-foot ladders, jumping from tall buildings into hand-held nets. After that there were written examinations. Southern survived all these hurdles and he got the job — $98 a month, instant affluence. He bought a 1925 touring car and started treating his young family to unheard-of extravagances, like a holiday in Vancouver.

What rescued most Canadians from the Depression was the war. Southern enlisted in the Royal Canadian Air Force in 1939, and spent the war as a firefighter on 19 different RCAF bases in Canada. He even fought a fire on the site of what is now ATCO's industrial park — "we made a good save," he says, "with only minor damage to a hangar lean-to."

After the war he returned to the Fire Department with a burning urge to get into something better. "I was going crazy in the Fire Department," he recalls. "My RCAF experiences of command as fire chief, with 22 men under my control, made me feel that I had to get out on my own." The entrepreneurial itch had got him. He wanted a business of his own, and he tried several. First, using his RCAF savings and by scrounging scarce plumbing fixtures from RCAF buildings that were being torn down, he built and sold two bungalows, making $2,000 on the deal. He also sold electric signs and bookkeeping systems, then borrowed $2,000 and promptly lost it on a scheme to record weddings on a battery of primitive wire recorders.

98

In 1946, while on vacation in Vancouver, Southern noticed U-Haul utility trailers for rent in various service stations around town. It struck him as a good idea. With his wife's savings and a $1,200 bank loan that was co-signed by a fellow fireman named Slim Farch, Southern bought 15 trailers, assembled them in his spare time and placed them for rent at several service stations in Calgary. He called his company Alberta Trailer Hire. Because there was a Fire Department rule against moonlighting, he gave 40 percent of the company to his son Ron, then a husky 16-year-old who planned to be a doctor.

Southern didn't realize it at the time, but North America in 1946 was about to become the most rootless, most mobile society the world has ever seen. The era when a man could expect to die in the house where he was born had vanished, along with family servants, front porches and the foxtrot, in 1939. A new and ungracious world was beginning — a world of disposable houses, interchangeable suburbs, mass-produced bungalows, two cars in every garage and, frequently, a rolling summer cottage to tow behind them.

This new affluence made it necessary to exploit the world's resources at a rate undreamed of even in wartime. The search for oil and for metals impelled men and women to live in the world's empty regions. In 1947, the first big well came in at Leduc less than a day's drive from Don Southern's fire hall, and launched the great Alberta oil boom. In the world's capitals, policy makers were beginning to respond to a new strategic environment, in which one powerful nation could incinerate another in a matter of seconds. All these trends were accelerating in the postwar years, and all of them were destined to enrich Don Southern and ATCO Industries. But of course he didn't know it at the time; he was too busy selling and renting trailers, when he wasn't at the fire hall.

Within a year of starting the business, Southern had sold his house on Calgary's Tenth Avenue, bought a vacant lot at 805 Third Street Northeast, built a bungalow on the site, and centralized his trailer-hire business in his own back yard. The first office was a tarpaper shack built on the site from scrounged hardware and recycled lumber. By now he was branching out. He sold residential trailers on consignment, bought and resold newly built trailers from a Calgary firm called Mastercraft, and sold war-surplus trailers for a profit of $70 each. His son Ron, still in high school, was deeply involved in the business too; he sold trailers and greased them and delivered them and worried about them. In 1947 he went away to Edmonton to attend the University of Alberta, paying for his tuition with his own savings. When he returned to Calgary for Christmas holidays, his money was exhausted and the family had no more; every cent of profit they had was tied up in a 16-foot Schult trailer that stood, unsold, in Southern's back yard. Miraculously, someone came in and bought it between Christmas and New Year. "The money from that sale," says Don Southern, "not only paid the last half-year for Ron's college, but also looked after the company well until spring." Total revenues for the next three months were $9.

As the 1940s closed, Southern was successful enough to contemplate quitting his fire-hall job, and to be suffering from horrendous cash shortages. He was plowing all his profits into spare parts and new inventory, and he needed cash to carry him between the time he spent everything he had on a trailer, and the time he sold it. Bank loans were hard to come by ("The bankers used to hold handkerchiefs in front of their faces, as though I had the plague"), so Southern entered into an arrangement with a local businessman named Bill Cozart who loaned the company money and arranged retail financing, in return for half the profits.

Southern almost lost the company — which was now renamed Alberta Trailer Co. Ltd. — as a result of this arrangement. Cozart, at a time when Southern was desperately short of cash, issued an ultimatum: either sell me half the company for $11,000, or I'll withdraw my financial support and go into business myself. Southern pleaded for time, then scurried around buying as many trailers as he could lay hands on, while he still had the umbrella of Cozart's financing, and parked them in the back yards and driveways of various friends around town. Then he terminated the contract and, in an orgy of selling, paid off Cozart's loans in seven months. "We knew we were in a serious spot," Southern says, "but there was no way we were going to let outsiders into the company."

By late 1951, Southern had quit the Fire Department, opened a second trailer sales lot in Edmonton, and hired the company's first employee — E. N. (Slim) Farch, the same fireman who'd co-signed Southern's original $1,200 loan, and who later became president of ATCO Structures Pty. Ltd., an Australian subsidiary. Farch turned out to be a brilliant salesman. On one memorable day he sold seven trailers, everything on the Edmonton lot, between nine in the morning and two in the afternoon.

Suddenly, after five years of 18-hour days, parsimonious living and staying one jump ahead of the bank, it all came together. The nation's new affluence, and its ability to produce the goods that people wanted to buy, finally intersected; and Southern, still operating out of that squalid tarpaper shack on Third Street Northeast, awoke one morning to realize that he was the proprietor of the biggest, busiest trailer company in Western Canada. By now it had offices — or, more accurately, vacant lots with trailers parked on them — in Regina, Edmonton, Fort St. John and Prince George, as well as in Calgary. It sold as many trailers as it could lay hands on. On a few great days it would clear as much as $7,000 a day. One day in 1953 someone phoned Southern and offered to buy the business for $250,000.

Southern was strongly tempted: "To me it was an awful lot of money." But before he made a decision, he had to consult with his partner, his son Ron, who had been given 40 percent of the business and, even during high school and university, had been doing at least 40 percent of the work. Ron, at that point, was 23 years old, married, and starting his final year of university. He'd taken two years of premedical studies, and two years of medical school, and he was still torn between medicine and business. He'd grown up in a household where money, or the lack of it, was a constant topic. He'd displayed entrepreneurial tendencies as early as the age of eight, when he'd bought some gelatin capsules at the drugstore, painted them, placed a ball-bearing inside each, and sold them at the Calgary Stampede as Mexican jumping beans. In his early teens he'd organized some classmates into a team that mowed lawns and weeded gardens in Calgary's Mount Royal district, an arrangement that netted him 10 cents per hour for each boy he hired. Since then he'd become one of Alberta Trailer's best salesmen, and had developed a growing inclination to express his own views on how the company should be run. "I was raised in an atmosphere where there was always this striving to accomplish," says Ron, "and it was always connected to a money reward."

"I can't figure out why Ron had this bee in his bonnet to be a doctor," says Cam Richardson, who knew him in high school and is now ATCO's senior vice-president in charge of finance. "He was an all-American boy — sports, girls, football, basketball, hockey, the whole bit. And he was always telling me about the trailer business, always figuring the angles. Yes, Ron always had a certain affinity for making a buck."

Ron had wanted to become a doctor since his early teens. But the more involved he became in the business, the more it occupied his thoughts. By his final year, when the $250,000 offer walked in the door, he'd almost made up his mind. He told his father: "Wait until I finish. Then I'll decide whether or not I'm coming into the business." Already he had plans for making the company grow into much more than a retailer of trailers, and he suspected that $250,000 was too low a price for the kind of potential he had in mind. "I guess I'd already made up my mind by that time," says Ron. "But I wanted to finish my fourth year and get my BSc., just so nobody could call me a dropout." That spring, with his degree in his pocket, Ron joined the company.

This was a crucial development in ATCO's history. It seems to be an inescapable fact of the entrepreneurial process that it takes different *kinds* of people to run a company at different stages of its growth. Don Southern was approaching his mid-40s. With little education but with an obsessive desire to afford all the things he and his family never had, he'd built a business that was grossing $1 million a year. He was more than satisfied with what he'd built. He also knew the company was operating on a very thin cash margin, and could be wiped out overnight by a single incautious decision. He knew how to preserve what he'd built. But people who know the company are unanimous that, if Ron Southern hadn't come into the business when he did, ATCO wouldn't be the multinational giant it is today.

At first, there was no formal agreement on who would run the company. But, says Ron: "There was a sort of natural evolution of me taking over more and more of the decision-making process."

It may have been natural, but it wasn't smooth. The office staff in the tarpaper shack — by now expanded to a building the size of a two-car garage — became accustomed to hearing father and son, closeted in a tiny office behind plywood partitions that relayed every sound, shouting at each other and slamming their fists on the desk. "In those days," says Cam Richardson, who sat in the outer office and found it hard to concentrate on his balance sheets, "Ron was a yeller. And his father always had been. So they used to plain and simple shout it out every once in a while. See, the old man is the kind of guy who has to have his four bits' worth. And Ron is the kind of guy who, if he's brought in to run something — well, he has to *run* it."

Two years after he joined the business full-time, in 1956, Ron and his father had their longest, loudest-ever shouting match. Neither man can remember what precipitated it, but the confrontation ended with the elder Southern yelling at his son: "All right, godammit, *you* run it!"

"And you know," says Ron with a slight wonderment, "he was as good as his word. He took a year's sales trip around the world — Africa, Australia, everywhere — and left me at home to run the show. Look: we were no different from any father and son. There's love and respect, yes, but there's also animosity. But the bittersweet thing about my relationship with my father is that, at a time when he was still a relatively young man, he gave me, a very young person, the opportunity to take that company and run it. What he gave me was my manhood and my ability as a manager. It was a great sacrifice for him, and it was the greatest act of love he could have given me."

Even before he assumed formal control as president, with his father stepping up to board chairman, Ron Southern had helped make the company's first major decision: to manufacture trailers as well as sell them. (In fact, there have been only four such decisions in the last 25 or so years — crucial, risk-laden determinations of which way the company should go — and Ron Southern made all four. We'll come to the other three later. If those decisions hadn't been made, and if they hadn't been right, the company would have stopped growing, or perhaps even have been squeezed out by the growing competition in the house-trailer business.)

The decision to go into manufacturing happened more or less by accident. The elder Southern, in the late 1940s, had agreed to build a house trailer for a young geophysicist. He spent a week hammering it together and sold it for a profit of exactly $71. Since he was already making a $70 profit on the war-surplus trailers he was selling, he reasoned that manufacturing, which paid him $1 for a week's hard work, was a fool's game. "I vowed then," says Don, "never to manufacture."

And so, when an oil-drilling company approached Slim Farch in Edmonton in 1953, asking him to build seven mobile bunkhouses that would be stronger and warmer than conventional trailers, Farch went ahead — without checking with the Southerns in Calgary. He hoped to make $2,000 on each of the seven units. But when the trailers were delivered and all the costs were tallied up, the total profit came to only $3,000. It wasn't good, but it was good enough to persuade the Southerns to enter into a partnership agreement with a small Edmonton cabinet-making shop, run by one Joe Semotiuk, to start building industrial trailers. With the oil boom in full swing, and with industrial customers complaining that conventional trailers weren't warm enough or strong enough to meet their requirements, manufacturing finally seemed like a feasible proposition. Southern and Semotiuk leased a concrete-block building in Edmonton, formed a jointly owned company called Roadway Industries Ltd., and started building. The first year's operations proved what Ron Southern and Slim Farch had been urging for years; the new company sold $250,000 worth of industrial trailers, and finished its first year with a profit of $17,000. In the second year of operations came the first big order — by far the biggest sale of any kind that the company had made to date: an order for 68 units from a pipeline construction company. Everyone worked close to the point of exhaustion that year. Wives sometimes used to deliver hot suppers to their men at the plant. Don Southern can remember racing around at 7 a.m. one winter morning, hauling beds into a newly built bunkhouse, its paint still wet, that was due for delivery at 8 a.m.

The toughest blow that winter was a fire. The gas heater exploded in Roadway's factory, the building filled with flames and, by the time firemen brought the blaze under control an hour later, the roof was gone. Only a dozen or so of the bunkhouses had been built and, by the time Don Southern arrived from Calgary, the customer was already threatening to take its order elsewhere. The Southerns "guaranteed their lives away" and managed to keep the order. Semotiuk built a temporary roof out of wood and canvas, installed temporary heaters, and kept production going. Southern, meanwhile, opened a second factory in a disused RCAF hangar at Airdrie, a few miles north of Calgary, where 40 buildings of the 68-unit order were completed. It was a frantic, heart-breaking winter, but the order was delivered on time. "I've never been in a theatre of war," says Don Southern, "but I think the supreme efforts shown then must have been the same as a warring nation would show after a bombing and burn-out."

Money was needed to set up the Airdrie plant and, when Semotiuk offered to buy out the ATCO half-interest in Roadway for $25,000, Southern agreed. "He might have been a millionaire today if he'd stuck with the team," Southern muses.

The Airdrie plant, like so many of ATCO's early ventures, was put together by scrounging, improvising and making-do. Wisps of straw still clung to the rafters, since a farmer had been using the building for storing hay. There was no sewer, only an outhouse. The nearest phone was at a neighboring farm, three miles away. There was a coal furnace that had to be stoked constantly, a shortage of drinking water, and frequent power failures. Airdrie, at the start, was about as primitive as a manufacturing plant can be. But the plant had one asset that made up for all the deficiencies: Jerry Kiefer.

Kiefer had grown up in the Ruhr Valley and, as a teen-ager used to walk 40 miles through a devastated industrial landscape to fetch a bag of potatoes. He emigrated to Canada, found a job in a sash and door factory, and met Don Southern when his employer sent Kiefer on an off-hours assignment to repair some windows in Southern's house. Southern started using him for various odd jobs, like adding a new wing to the tarpaper shack on Third Street, and building a trailer with fold-down eaves that was used as the office building in ATCO's Regina trailer sales lot. By 1955, Kiefer was doing so much work for the company it was cheaper to hire him. He became ATCO's first production manager, and now sits on the board as vice-president in charge of production.

At the Airdrie plant, Kiefer worked like a maniac, often sleeping in the eight-by-18 office building he'd erected beside the hanger, conveniently near the outhouse. Orders for industrial buildings, either for rental units or for straight sales, were beginning to pour in. A dozen companies wanted drilling camps all at once. Orders from highways departments for on-site construction shacks began arriving in the mail. Power companies, pipeline construction firms, geophysical crews, mining companies, even a few hard-pressed school boards, became customers. Canadians were moving to where the resources were, and ATCO, to its vast surprise, found itself becoming not only the largest, but virtually the only firm anywhere that was able to supply the instant housing these people needed.

Kiefer frantically expanded the Airdrie site, occupying and converting one empty RCAF building after another. At times, it seemed as though he was manufacturing buildings to manufacture other buildings. The other parts of ATCO's business were expanding too. The trailer-rental business was now a nation-wide operation. The property on Third Street Northeast, with the chairman and founder still living in a bungalow next door, was absurdly overcrowded: at the peak there were eight ATCO-built office trailers on the site, with accountants, purchasing agents and clerks working out of each other's laps. "There were no communications problems in those days," says Cam Richardson, "because everybody knew what everybody else was doing — we couldn't help hearing them do it." As the 1950s came to an end, ATCO had a payroll of at least 100 — there were 50 office staff alone — and had developed a feast-or-famine sales pattern: because of the vagaries of the construction industry, there were either too many orders, or not enough. ATCO even had a Telex now, to link nearly a dozen offices scattered around the country.

But it was still a small company, and it was still a desperately insecure one. Ron Southern, who functioned as chief salesman along with everything else but production, had pushed the company to limits that his father hadn't dreamed possible — and which still gave the older man nightmares. "Our financial planning consisted of going to the bank every month and asking for a bigger overdraft," says Richardson. "We were always operating close to the edge. I mean, if we were late paying our bills some months, it wasn't because the accounts department was inefficient. It was because we plain and simple didn't have the money."

One morning late in 1959, a message came over the Telex that was to transform the company, but almost sank it in the process.

The message was from a catering firm in Seattle, Universal Services, with which ATCO had done business in the past. WE HAVE A BIG CLIENT, is roughly how the message read, COME ON DOWN. Ron Southern was on a sales trip in Vancouver at the time, and flew to Seattle to find out what was up. The following day he Telexed a report back to Calgary, and Cam Richardson can remember people gathering excitedly around the machine as the message clattered out: UNIVERSAL'S CLIENT IS BOEING, read Southern's message, AM STAYING EXTRA DAY.

Boeing had received the military contract for construction of dozens of "hardened" Minuteman missile sites around the U.S., mostly in desert areas of the Southwest. It meant that not hundreds, but thousands of people would be living for months on end in localities populated chiefly by lizards. Boeing badly needed housing for these people, and they weren't interested in spartan accommodations. Most of the on-site people would be highly paid aerospace specialists. To keep them happy, and keep them on the job, Boeing wanted all the comforts of a Houston suburb — television, ice cream cones, swimming pools, filet mignon, color-coordinated interiors, movies every Friday, cold beer, everything.

While Southern was homing in on Boeing, the company, it turned out, was homing in on ATCO. A Boeing procurement executive heard about ACTO by talking over his back fence with a neighbor who had worked on ATCO-housed construction projects in Alaska. Boeing had a serious procurement problem; and it was discovering, to its surprise, that practically the only company in the world with the capability of solving it was this little outfit up in Calgary.

Within a matter of weeks, Southern got the contract — ATCO's biggest sale to date, worth several million dollars. A Boeing official had visited the plant at Airdrie, taken one look at the converted barn-hangar, the primitive facilities, the wooden privy that still stood out behind and said: "Ron, we're going to swamp you with work." Southern replied: "We'll all have hammers in our hands and we'll build them in the fields — but we'll deliver on time."

The elder Southern was horrified. How could an outfit like ATCO possibly meet this commitment? He knew that cost over-runs or unexpected delays could, in a matter of months, destroy the company he'd worked so long to build. "I was conservative," he says, "because I felt I'd *made* mine. But Ron was out to make his, and out to do better than his old man."

Getting the contract and getting it nailed down turned out to be two different things. Ron Southern had verbal assurances that ATCO would be getting the business. But dealing with Boeing, he discovered, "was like dealing with a government." There were miles of red tape to unravel, unheard-of requirements to meet, endless questionnaires to complete, performance guarantees to negotiate, specifications to pin down. Boeing, in accordance with U.S. Defense Department regulations, wanted competitive bids and, since there was no competition, encouraged small trailer manufacturers in Seattle to enter the contest. Most of ATCO's key people took up residence in Seattle for six months, spending a terrifying amount of money and, as far as they could see, getting no closer to signed, sealed, completed orders that would allow them to start work.

One evening about six months after his initial contact with Boeing, Southern came home to his wife in their rented Seattle apartment and said: "Marg, I think we're going to lose everything." Marg said: "Ron, you can't give up. Go see Mr. Hurst." Bud Hurst was in charge of procurement for the project. At 6:15 the next morning, Southern was at his door. Hurst, still in his pajamas, invited him in for coffee. Southern explained how Boeing's red tape was on the point of sinking the company. Hurst said he'd look into it. That same night, Southern came home with three orders in his pocket for $2.5 million worth of buildings.

That day marked the dividing point. Behind it was the hole-in-the-wall company founded by a Calgary fireman. Ahead of it was a multinational corporation run by his son. Getting the Boeing contract, and completing it on time, was an incredible learning experience. And, once the company had mastered the intricacies of American defense procurement, other orders came almost automatically: Philco, Lockheed, the U.S. Army, the Atomic Energy Commission. ATCO worked with Boeing for nearly seven years and, by the time the Minuteman program was complete, had sold $12 million worth of structures. It meant hiring hundreds of new people but, more important, it transformed the company's style. Purchasing departments, management manuals, organized procedures, accounting controls — all the administrative machinery of a large business came into being through the Boeing contracts; not merely because ATCO was growing and needed them, but also because Boeing, in line with the strict procurement procedures laid down by the Pentagon, insisted on it. "We didn't realize it at the time," says Cam Richardson, "but we were in the process of developing an industry."

They were also developing a rather amazing chief executive. The Boeing contract gave Ron Southern a vision of success, of the big time, and of what ATCO might become; his father was a tarpaper-shack man; Ron was thinking board room. "He doesn't do anything, not anything, with a casual, relaxed approach," says one of his associates. "I don't see why he doesn't get ulcers. He expects everybody to be as intense as he is, which is unrealistic. Not everybody's built that way."

Southern today is the image of the sort of executive who is customarily referred to as "dynamic" and "hard-driving." He has that clean, cleft-chinned look of the football-player-turned-corporate-statesman. "I'm a team player," he says, using the usual sports-page metaphors. "I found out very early that if you can get people to work together, there's no end to what you can accomplish."

"He's arrogant and cocky to the point that he upsets people," says one of his former associates. "It's his youth, I guess. If he were 30 years older, people might accept it. I'll give you an example. He's got to catch a chartered flight to somewhere, and his secretary drives him to the airport and drops him at the commercial terminal by mistake. His plane is at the other end of the airport, but does Ron Southern take a taxi? No, he insists that the chartered plane taxi all the way across the airport and pick up him where he was." There are lots of other stories about Southern's legendary *chutzpah.*

Much of corporate life consists of running to stand still: the endless round of day-to-day decisions that keep you one step ahead of the banks, and your suppliers, and your customers. But once in a while, a chief executive makes a *big* decision — initiates a crucial change of direction that determines where his company will be, or won't be, in five or 10 years. Often, the chief executive makes these decisions without realizing it — or without realizing that they're crucial. That's how ATCO made its first big decision: to go into manufacturing. Later on, it went after the Boeing contract. Seen in retrospect, it was an enormous plunge that could have failed. Because it succeeded, it transformed the character of the company.

Ron Southern was instrumental in both these decisions. In the following decade, he made two more. In the early 1960s, realizing that ATCO was becoming dangerously dependent on the boom-and-bust cycles of Canadian resource industries, he decided to diversify. He wanted to increase the range of ATCO's products, instead of specializing in portable industrial buildings. And he wanted to sell them all over the world, instead of just in Canada and the U.S.

That decision — really, it was a series of decisions — carried ATCO to a new stage of growth. By 1968, the year ATCO went public, sales were more than $42 million. By 1975 revenues had grown to nearly $165 million, and the company had become a sizeable bureaucracy. That, in turn, led to Southern's fourth major decision: to decentralize the company's management. During the 1960s, with subsidiaries sprouting around the world, with some executives flying a million miles a year, with ATCO portable buildings installed in such diverse locations as the Sahara Desert and the South Pole, the company's head office became as crowded as the old tarpaper shack had once been. There was a danger of Too Many Chiefs. So Southern reshuffled the ATCO empire into a string of semi-autonomous subsidiaries, each with its own goals and methods. At the same time, he standardized product lines — made ATCO's industrial housing more of an assembly-line item. "Before," explained an ATCO executive, "if a guy wanted wheels on the roof, we'd say: "Sure you can have wheels on the roof — where do you want them?" Well, hell, with that kind of custom-tailoring, we'd reached the point where we were so tied up in red tape, our lines of communication were so long, that we couldn't go anywhere. So we standardized."

Even with standardization, by 1974 ATCO Industries Ltd. was involved in an astonishing variety of products. In Calgary and Edmonton, a subsidiary called Cedarglen Homes was building suburban bungalows. Another ATCO company, Superior Components Ltd., was supplying everything from motel furniture to heating ducts for mobile homes, from metal stable stalls for a horse barn on the Calgary Exhibition grounds to the lobby decor for Toronto's Hyatt Regency Hotel. An Australian subsidiary was producing structural steel for factory buildings. Canadian subsidiaries were manufacturing huge factory buildings that can be erected — and folded away — in six hours. What else? Flatbed trailers, cargo containers, foldaway shelters for the U.S. Army and mobile homes from factories in California, Idaho and Montreal, as well as Calgary.

But industrial housing still provided about half of ATCO's revenues. In this specialized field, ATCO isn't merely the leading competitor; it's practically the only one. At one point in 1973, school children in Libya were studying in ATCO portable classrooms; miners in Greenland were living in ATCO bunkhouses, and the mine's managers were living in equally portable three-bedroom bungalows. By now, the company considers it routine to erect what amounts to a small North American suburb, complete with movie theatre, church, bank, bowling alley and restaurant, in some God-forsaken outpost like Moomba, Australia. Some ATCO buildings are designed to house exotic items like swimming pools and computers — but all of them can be folded up and flown out whenever their owners choose. The postwar era gave us disposable diapers, disposable syringes, disposable towels and disposable marriages. But it was ATCO that gave us possibly the ultimate post-war phenomenon, the disposable village.

7

IAN BRUCE: 'WE JUST BUILT A LITTLE BOAT'

To understand Ian Bruce, the man who engineered the success of the Laser, which may turn out to be the world's most popular sailboat, you must understand that in 1954, when he was 21 and in imminent danger of flunking his engineering course at McGill, he dropped out of university to become a ballroom dancing instructor.

The Laser is a 14-foot fibreglass sailboat that is manufactured in Montreal by Bruce's company, Performance Sailcraft Inc. It is not a plaything. It is a boat that seasoned sailors respect. Because Lasers are so fast and so rewarding to sail, and because sailors around the world have bought so many of them, the design has been granted the status of an international class — and, what's more, a class that only Performance Sailcraft, or firms licensed by Performance Sailcraft, may manufacture. It is a sweet situation for a company to be in — roughly equivalent to being the only firm in the world permitted to manufacture baseballs for league competition. Bruce was 41 in 1975, and he'd spent several years of underpaid work developing the Laser. He'd sold more than 27,000 of them, and it was assumed in yacht-racing circles that by now he must be extremely rich. He wasn't. By 1975 his company had expanded worldwide, and had done it without piling up massive debts. But the company's *total* profit on the first 22,000 Lasers sold was about $11,000 — about 50 cents per boat.

It's true that, in the coming years, Ian Bruce and his associates may become very rich indeed. They've developed what amounts to the Model T of the yacht-racing world, and they've secured what amounts to a worldwide monopoly on its manufacture. But, like most entrepreneurs, Bruce isn't motivated by money. Instead, he dreams of other boats he'd like to build. His most powerful drive is simply to keep doing what interests him, which is the same inner-directed urgency that prompted him to drop out of McGill to become a dancing instructor.

Bruce moved in fairly stuffy circles in those days. He'd grown up in Jamaica and the Bahamas, where his English father was very much part of the local Establishment, and he'd spent six years at a WASP bastion, Trinity College School in Port Hope, Ontario. His milieu in Montreal included old TCS chums, his father's Westmount friends, the Royal St. Lawrence Yacht Club and the Alpha Delt house. So one can readily imagine the consternation of those who knew him. Here was this nice, easygoing, well-connected young man, absolutely nothing wrong with his background, suddenly turning up for work each afternoon at Dino's Dance Studio on St. Catherine Street. What possessed him? Dino's was one of those sad little upstairs emporiums with a record player in one corner and a clientele that consisted of the lonely, the elderly, the unattached, most of them attracted by some half-formed vision of glamour and ease and assurance. Bruce spent eight hours a day in this place at a guaranteed $20 a week. He served his first two months without pay, learning to be an instructor, wholly indifferent to the reactions of those who knew him. His name was dropped from certain invitation lists to deb dances. His fraternity brothers thought he'd turned queer. His father's friends from Westmount thought he'd become a gigolo.

What Bruce was becoming, in fact, was his own man. Engineering bored him, but that was the course his father had urged him to take. Most of the people he knew bored him too. "I was fed up with their stuffiness," he recalls. "I was fed up with fraternity dances, with the same type of upper-middle-class people, with everything always being so straight. I was beginning to itch a little bit. I was ready for a fling. And a fling was very hard to come by in the university society of those days."

No, the dance studio wasn't simply a young man's elaborate 1950s strategem to lose his virginity. Bruce really wanted to learn to dance well. As a teenager in Nassau, where his family had moved from Jamaica in 1945, he'd been part of the colony's sub-deb set, a small gang of Anglo-Caribbean rich kids who spent their winters at schools in England and Canada, and their summers home in Nassau, spearfishing together, waterskiing, attending well-chaperoned beach parties — and dancing on moonlit patios to some palm-court orchestra at the British Colonial Hotel. "When I look back on it, it was terribly romantic, a marvelous part of my life. We danced because it was fun. We never went out to drink. We danced hard and drank ginger ale all night because we'd be exhausted by 10 o'clock. Then, home to bed and out spearfishing the next morning at seven. That's how I grew up."

Bruce regarded ballroom dancing as an extension of athletics — a challenge, a skill he wanted to master. Growing up in the tropics, he'd acquired what can only be described as, yes, a natural sense of rhythm; and this sense of rhythm has given a theme to his life. It impelled him to spend that strange year as a dancing instructor. It later helped him to become a confident skier and one of the best sport sailors in the world, both of them activities in which rhythm is a central consideration. He still keeps a conga drum in his living room beside the fireplace, a reminder of the days when he'd sit in with calypso bands in Montreal. And one can even detect a certain rhythmic quality in his career as an entrepreneur — something easy and graceful about the way his company developed, something to do with timing.

"There's a big connection between sailing, skiing and ballroom dancing," Bruce says. "Any sport is well over 50 percent rhythm. If you've watched a good skier coming down a hill and watched a good dancer on the floor, you can't help but notice the similarity of body movements. It's the same with sailing. In dancing, you can't turn unless you're balanced to turn. You can't jibe in sailing unless your body's in the right position. Basically, steering a boat upwind is a matter of moving the tiller within a range of about three inches. And within that three inches of movement, what you do with the tiller determines whether you come first or last in a race. Anyone I've ever known who was good at sports was just loaded with rhythm."

A few months before he became a dance instructor, Bruce also discovered sailing. He was in love with both activities, and he set out to master both with the same dogged persistence. At Dino's dance studio, he quickly became a star instructor, specializing in teaching couples. He told Dino that he refused to sell lessons to his clients. Even so, by the end of the year he had the highest renewal rate of all Dino's 20-odd instructors. "I simply taught hard and taught well," he says. By the end of that year, some of his friends were beginning to acknowledge that perhaps he hadn't gone completely mad. Some of his parents' Westmount friends even enrolled for lessons; the thing was becoming almost respectable.

Sailing inspired the same kind of commitment. Bruce's father had bought him a sailboat when he was 14. It sat unused beside a wharf all one summer; in those days, Bruce was more interested in spearfishing. But in the summer of 1953, a McGill friend named Kirk Cooper asked Bruce to crew in an International 14. "What happened," he says, "is that we were in a race, and I'd never been in a race in a sailboat before. I just got turned on by this form of competition. I fell in love with the sport overnight." He used $300 that his father had given him for not taking up smoking and, with Kirk Cooper, bought an International 14 of his own. Within a year, he was on his way to becoming an Olympic-calibre sailor.

There was a pattern emerging here: Bruce, even at 21, was superb at things he wanted to do, but dreadful at things he didn't want to do. His engineering course at McGill was a series of academic disasters. His grades had been falling when he decided to spend a year at Dino's Dance Studio. And when he returned to McGill for his fourth year of engineering, it got worse. Bruce simply wasn't interested in engineering. He was, however, interested in architecture. He was rooming with an old TCS schoolmate who was studying architecture; Bruce became his friend's understudy — reading his textbooks, helping him study for his architecture exams, helping build his friend's architectural models. He was also president of his fraternity and, based on his marks in the first year, president of the engineering honors society. But at the end of his fourth year, Bruce became the only honor society president in the history of McGill to flunk out of engineering. He hadn't studied, he hadn't attended classes. Some of his marks were among the lowest ever recorded in the engineering faculty.

By the time he received the grim news, Bruce was working as

a junior employee at Alcan Aluminum's plant in Wakefield, Quebec, just outside Ottawa. It started as a summer job, and Bruce did well enough that the company, even after it was known that he'd flunked out, asked him to stay on. Every evening he'd drive down to Ottawa and sail at the Britannia Yacht Club, sometimes crewing in International 14s with an Ottawa layer named Ward McKimm, who was later to become a key figure in Performance Sailcraft Inc. That was where he also met his future wife, Barbara. They were married in the spring of 1958.

Soon after their marriage, Bruce began thinking seriously about his career. He was nearly 26, a failed engineer with a gnawing creative urge. His boss, John Gnaedinger, knew he'd rise in the company. "But one fine day," he told Bruce, "you're going to walk through a door and there'll be a couple of jobs on the line. The other guys will have a degree and you won't. And you're going to be the one that loses out." He knew he'd never succeed as an engineer, and he felt it was now too late for architecture. Perhaps because he'd designed and built all the furniture in their newlywed apartment, Bruce began thinking about industrial design. He visited Syracuse University, one of the few institutions within a 300-mile radius of Ottawa that offered a degree course in industrial design — and suddenly felt as though he'd Come Home. "I just walked through the door of that place, and I said to myself — 'That's it! There it is! That's everything I should have been doing at McGill. It's all stuck up on the walls, it's in the clay models in the corner, it's all there.' Incredible."

The Bruces changed apartments 14 times in the next 30 months: a few semesters in Syracuse, then back to his old job with Alcan in the summer, then back to Syracuse. Everything they owned could be packed into their 1957 Ford station wagon. If it didn't fit, they left it on the sidewalk. One semester, when Barbara was working in the university's admissions office, she found the letter of recommendation that had helped her husband get into the school, sent by the dean of engineering at McGill. "He wrote an extremely strong letter," says Bruce. "He acknowledged that I'd flunked, but said that if Ian Bruce ever gets into a program that interests him, he'll probably lead the class." The dean was right. Bruce graduated *magna cum laude* from Syracuse in 1961, at the head of his class. He was almost 30, and by this time he'd amassed a frightening pile of debts, debts it took him nearly 15 years to repay.

Back in Montreal after graduation, he took a job at $75 a week with Julien Hebert, who ran a small design studio. It was a four-man shop, but very active. They designed, among many other things, Alcan's foil box and the logo for Expo 67, a circle made up of little stick-figures. Late in 1963, Bruce and two of his colleagues at Hebert's, Marcel Girard and Jacques Garabedian, formed their own design partnership. To launch the business, each of them went to a nearby Bank of Montreal branch to borrow $200. By this time he was 30, a new father, still drawing $75 a week in salary, and he still hadn't reduced his debts, which amounted to several times his annual income. "Financially, I was a disaster," says Bruce. "But it didn't worry me at all, because I knew that those things I put my mind to — sailing, design school, whatever — I'd gotten there. So now I figured it was time to start making a success of my financial life and my design career."

The new firm opened at the right time. The planning for Expo 67 was a windfall for many design firms, and it helped stimulate business in other areas. The firm of Girard, Bruce, Garabedian and Associates expanded rapidly. They designed a theme pavilion at Expo, they designed the signs for Place Bonaventure, they designed a line of furniture for Simmons that won nine design awards, they designed the familiar blue-and-green paint job for the Voyageur Colonial buses. When Expo finished, only a few Montreal design firms survived the bust that followed the boom. Bruce's firm was one of them.

By this time, however, he was embarked on a second, parallel career. Ever since his first race at the age of 21, he'd been a dedicated sailor. By now he was one of Canada's best. In 1959, when he was still at design school in Syracuse, he won the Canadian trials for the Finn class, a single-handed centreboard boat with a single sail, and represented Canada at the Rome Olympics in 1960. In 1967, he was captain of a team of four Canadians — Ward McKimm was another — who sailed against four-man British and American International 14 teams in England. Bruce sailed his own boat — he'd paid $2,400 for it to an English builder — and Ward McKimm steered another International 14. Later on that same trip, after the team racing was over, Bruce entered the series for the Prince of Wales Trophy at Cowes and, with 90 other boats behind him, won one race by an entire leg of the course. He won the trophy; it meant he was the world's top International 14 sailor.

Bruce didn't win that trophy merely by managing the tiller more skilfully than any of the other 90-odd competitors. Much of his success was due to the boat's design. The International 14 is what's known as a "development class", which means that competitors are free to make whatever design improvements they choose, so long as they fall within certain design limitations (such as the 14-foot hull length) enforced by the International Yacht Racing Union (IYRU), the governing body of the sport. Bruce's boat was built by a small English builder, with a hull of moulded plywood designed by Bruce Kirby, a Canadian-born designer. Ian Bruce used his combined experience as an Olympic-class sailor, and as an industrial designer, to make a few improvements of his own. He designed his own centreboard, for instance, and installed an extremely flexible mast. It was this precise configuration of hull design, rigging, mast and centreboard, plus Bruce's skill as a helmsman, that won the trophy at Cowes. Through a fortunate combination of the talents of several people, in other words, Bruce now owned the fastest International 14 in the world.

When he returned to Canada after the Cowes event, Bruce decided to start building International 14s. The decision was made casually, over lunch at Montreal's Playboy Club, with a sailing friend named André Julien. There were only about 1,000 International 14s in the world, most of them built slowly and carefully by small British firms. "The people who build 14s," says Bruce, "build them basically for love. But there were so few of them that the class was in danger of disappearing in Canada. With the design skills I had, and with my knowledge of the craft, I felt I could put together a 14 in fibreglass that would be very competitive in races, and would maintain the presence of the class in Canada. It really wasn't done for any other reason. It was strictly hobby stuff. I just figured I could be a good guy, and have some fun doing it."

So Bruce set to work designing a fibreglass replica of his own plywood boat. He made no changes to the hull that Bruce Kirby had designed. But, working with clay, he designed a new interior. Then he and Julien formed a partnership, and found a few friends who agreed to buy a boat if it ever reached production, and to underwrite the tooling costs if it never got that far. The downside risk for each of the 10 guarantors wasn't large: $170.

They found a fibreglass subcontractor in suburban La Salle to manufacture the boats from the moulds that Bruce had designed. Over the winter of 1967-68, the partnership built 17 boats. Bruce and Julien installed the rigging themselves after office hours. The new boat was well received by International 14 sailors. It was, after all, a virtual replica of what was then the fastest 14 in the world. By the summer of 1968, when they'd received orders for another 35 boats, Bruce and Julien decided to manufacture the hulls themselves. They hired Peter Hans, who'd been the foreman at the subcontracting firm, leased 4,000 square feet of space in a factory building near Dorval Airport, incorporated Performance Sailcraft Inc. and started work over the winter on the second batch. Julien was running his family's paint company, and Bruce was still busy with his design company downtown. But Performance Sailcraft, which had started out as a hobby began to swallow more and more of Bruce's time.

Throughout this period, they'd been working closely with Bruce Kirby, the designer. Kirby was a newspaperman and avid part-time sailor who'd grown up in Ottawa. In his days as a copy editor on the Montreal Star, he used to spend his spare time doodling boat designs on sheets of copy paper. In 1965, Kirby had taken a job in the U.S. as editor of a yachting magazine, and continued designing boats. He was totally self-taught, but his work was becoming known wherever 14s were sailed. And when, late in 1969, Kirby developed an improved design for the International 14 – the Kirby Mark V – Bruce decided to build it. By this time, the young company had also received an order from the Royal St. Lawrence Yacht Club to build 15 training dinghies for use by the club's junior members. It may not sound like much, but for a man with a full-time job already, it represented a killing commitment. "I was spending more time in the boat-building operation than I was at work," says Bruce. "It's a fantastic load to ask your family to carry. I don't think I'm different from anybody who's gone through the process of starting a company. You pay a price, in terms of your family and your body."

Bruce was fed up. They'd built fewer than 50 boats, and cleared a few thousand dollars. The experience had shown that building a few boats at a time takes too much time and produces too little revenue. In December 1969, Bruce phoned Kirby in Connecticut and poured out his troubles. "I told him I was going to pack the whole thing in unless I had a design which I thought could be mass-produced." What Bruce had in mind, he told Kirby, was a car-top boat that *looked* like a boat, not a glorified surfboard; an inexpensive little boat that families could take to the beach or leave at the cottage. The conversation turned out to be historic. As they spoke, Kirby sketched a design on a scratch-pad, a doodle that was to become the Laser, and which now hangs, framed, on the wall by Kirby's desk. Two weeks later he mailed off working drawings to Montreal.

Nothing happened until late in the summer of 1970. Bruce was frantically busy, running his design business all day, then driving out to Pointe Claire to build boats until two or three in the morning. Late in August he received a phone call from Kirby. His boating magazine was sponsoring a regatta in mid-October for small off-the-beach boats costing $1,000 or less. "If you're going to do anything with my design," said Kirby, "you'd better have the boat ready for the Teacup Regatta."

So Bruce and his production foreman, Peter Hans, pulled Kirby's drawings out of a desk drawer and set to work. They started from absolute scratch on September 1. The process of building wooden mock-ups of the hull and deck, then making fibreglass moulds from them, was slow and painstaking, but it went smoothly, almost eerily so. "All the way along, there was never a hitch," says Bruce. "That's most unusual. I mean, we've always had hitches for some reason in every tooling program we've gone through. For some reason, this one never got hung up anywhere along the line."

As the deadline approached, the pressure mounted. Bruce and Peter Hans worked 240 straight hours between them, laying up the hull and deck of the world's first Laser — although at that point it didn't have a name. The job was finished by six on a Saturday morning in October. Two hours later, they glued the hull and deck together, and the rest of the workmen went home. "I'd been awake for 72 straight hours. Then I had an hour's nap on some slabs of foam at the plant. Then I got up and started putting on the fittings. A customer wandered in around noon, looking for some spare part, and he pitched in to help. By midnight Saturday we had the boat rigged. So we hoisted it onto the roof of my car — by now I'd been up for 82 or 84 hours — and we drove to Toronto in shifts." The regatta was due to start on Monday morning at Lake Geneva, Wisconsin. Around eight Sunday morning, Bruce and his customer, Evert Bastet (who'd agreed on the spot to come along), arrived in Toronto, where they picked up the boat's Kirby-designed sails from sailmaker Hans Fogh. Then they continued on to Chicago, a 500-mile drive, and arrived at Lake Geneva to register their newborn boat by 6 p.m. Then, gratefully, Bruce collapsed in a motel.

They'd finished the boat, and the competition on Monday was almost an anticlimax. The Laser, with Hans Fogh at the helm, performed beautifully. But Fogh wasn't satisfied. That night he recut the sail and, in Tuesday's races, the Laser performed even better.

In the series, out of a field of about 20, the Laser tied with another boat called a Banshee. Fair enough, but Bruce, who'd spent 15 years of his life hanging around yacht clubs, could sense something important: the reaction of the experienced sailors who saw the Laser. "It was one of the only really new things on the beach. No one had ever seen or heard of it before. It had a purple hull and a pink deck — I'd done that on purpose. People started talking about it — 'Hey, did you see that boat with the pink deck out there?' — and the reaction of the knowledgeable members of the fraternity was so positive that I thought: 'Right — this thing has really got the potential to go somewhere.' It was just a gut reaction I had — a feeling that here was something that could really be promoted to the *established* sailor, which was a complete departure from what I'd asked Kirby to design. The cottage market is what I'd asked for. And, all the time we were producing the boat, I kept asking myself, 'How am I going to promote this boat to the cottage market?' because that takes millions of dollars.

"But Kirby, by his own admission, designed a boat that came out hotter than he anticipated. And all of a sudden, instead of it being just another nice cottage boat, it was — well, the reaction was, 'Jesus! That boat is *fast!*' I mean, the boat attracted a whole different segment of the market from the one I'd anticipated —the experienced sailor. And by the time we'd put our boat back on the roofrack after that regatta was over, I'd done a 180-degree shift in my mind. I knew exactly what to do. 'If I can really put this boat to bed,' I told myself, 'I think we can attract the very competent sailor. And there's a man I can talk to for a minimum number of dollars.' "

Putting the boat to bed involved another few weeks of tinkering: testing the mast placement, making minor modifications to the sail and hull. On a bitterly cold day in November 1970, Bruce and Kirby and Fogh sailed a modified Laser on the St. Lawrence, only a few days before freeze-up. "As the light died, the first snowfall started," Bruce recalls. "And we took her out of the water and said, 'That's it.' And we haven't touched the design since."

A few weeks later, they took four Lasers to the New York Boat Show. For boat manufacturers, this is like making a debut at Carnegie Hall. The Laser was an immediate success. One dealer from Chicago, Jack Gorman, ordered 100 on the spot. "To me it was a good business venture," Gorman later explained. "The boat filled a screaming need in the market for a light, high-performance boat." When Bruce returned to Montreal from the boat show, he leased a factory building three times as large, and started building boats. By May 1971, they were building 20 Lasers a week, and orders were backed up until August. Performance Sailcraft built 800 boats during that first fiscal year and grossed $432,000. The Laser, at last, was launched.

Unless you're a sailor, it's difficult to explain what makes the Laser so attractive. There are other small, high-performance sailing dinghies — the Finn is one — and there are scores of off-the-beach boats, such as the Sunfish, which have sold in large numbers. Most of these off-the-beach boats, however, have been marketed like snowmobiles or sports cars, to a family recreational market.

But the Laser is a boat that experienced sailors can relate to. Scott Warrener, Performance Sailcraft's production manager and now one of its four shareholders, was a small-boat sailor who worked as a systems engineer for General Motors when Bruce approached him to run the plant. The offer was less than dazzling in financial terms: Bruce proposed that Warrener work for nothing for 10 months; and then, if he wished, he could buy 15 percent of the company for about $1,400. Bruce took him to the Royal St.

Lawrence Yacht Club to see one of the early Lasers. Warrener took one look and said: "I'll run your plant."

The boat's design, obviously, was the chief ingredient of its appeal. It looks like a fast, demanding, single-handed racing machine, and it performs like one. "In retrospect," says Bruce, "I suppose it shouldn't be surprising that we turned out a hot boat. I got the best designer to do the lines, I got the best sailmaker to do the sail and to steer the thing at that first regatta, and I figured I was as good as anybody to do the tooling and the fitting of the mast and the rigging and putting the thing together. I mean, think of it: three Olympic helmsmen go to work on something that's only 14 feet long, and between us we've had something like 25 or 30 years of racing experience at the very top international level. So I guess it isn't really surprising that we turned out a hot boat."

But other hot boats haven't sold nearly as well. What distinguished the Laser from the others was Bruce's decision, made shortly after he returned from that first regatta on Lake Geneva, to promote the Laser as a rigid one-design boat. Most international yachting competition consists of what Bruce calls "an armaments race." Yachtsmen compete not so much on the basis of their skill as helmsmen, but on technological superiority. In most competitive classes, subtle — and usually costly — improvements in hull and sail design are what win races.

Bruce's crucial concept was his decision to produce a competitive sailboat in which *no* variations would be allowed. Every Laser in the world would be exactly like every other Laser, so their owners would be competing on the basis of skill, not equipment. "The Laser," wrote a small-boat sailor named Norm Freeman in an admiring article in *Yachting*, "gives us a chance to use basic sailing skills that every racing sailor must possess, whether he sails dinghies or 50-footers, in order to win races with any degree of consistency. The phrase, 'simple but sophisticated' must apply to the Laser as to no other class that I have sailed . . ."

Bruce made one other crucial decision at the New York boat show, although it didn't seem crucial at the time. He decided to trust the dealers who wanted to sell his boat. Most Laser dealers are respected racing sailors themselves. "That first summer, we just played the country cousin," says Bruce. "We knew how to build the boat and the dealers were going to tell us how to market it. The key was, we listened to people who knew more about marketing than we did. From then on, the thing went like lightning, and mostly by word-of-mouth." By 1975, Lasers were being sold by 175 dealers across North America. Bruce won't appoint a dealer unless all the other dealers in adjacent territories agree, and he's deliberately made the territories large.

Most new manufacturing companies stagger from payroll to payroll, with their entrepreneurs frantically scrabbling for cash to keep the thing going. Performance Sailcraft didn't follow this pattern. The company's capital investment was quite small. The plant set up after the New York Boat show cost less than $20,000 to put into operation, and, at the beginning, the company was able to sell boats as fast as it could produce them. Still, there were crises. The first came in August 1971, six months after production began, when President Nixon, in a bid to reduce the U.S. balance-of-payments imbalance, announced a 10 percent tax surcharge on imports. Since most of Performance Sailcraft's production was being shipped to the U.S., the effect of the announcement was abrupt and frightening. The next day, dealers phoned to cancel their orders. The surcharge was to be temporary, and the dealers were worried that, by ordering during the period when the surcharge was in force, they'd be paying an extra $60 per boat, and then would have to absorb that increase themselves in the spring after the surcharge was removed.

Bruce was in a bind. "We knew that if we went into the spring without boats, that was the end of the Laser. Somebody else, having seen our success that first summer, would jump on the bandwagon and absolutely wipe us out. The only reason somebody didn't jump in is that we'd priced the boat so low — $695. They all thought we were crazy, that we'd be bankrupt in six months. We weren't."

So there was really no choice. Bruce decided to continue producing boats over the winter, even though the dealers weren't buying. To bridge the cash gap, he got a bank loan against the growing inventory. Ward McKimm, the Ottawa lawyer who'd sailed with Bruce at Cowes, also advanced a personal loan. By this time McKimm was a shareholder, with an increasing personal stake in the company. By 1975 he'd left his Ottawa law practice and joined the company.

Together, Bruce and McKimm developed a direction for the young company that was audacious in the extreme. They'd keep the price low, to discourage competition. They'd expand worldwide, with plants in several countries. And they'd invest money in the development of a class organization — an association of Laser owners promoted and financed by the company that builds them. And they'd finance all these things, if possible, with the cash-flow generated by the boats they built, and by loans from banks and shareholders. There were only four: Bruce and Julien with 37 percent each; McKimm and Warrener with 13 percent each.

Bruce and McKimm moved fast. In the summer of 1971, they made a deal with a California sailor and part-time boat builder named Don Trask: in return for 30 percent of his company, Trask got the right to build and sell Lasers in the western U.S., plus Hawaii, Guam and Mexico. In the fall of the same year, Bruce and McKimm flew to England, bought a factory building in Banbury, hired an Olympic sailor named Paul Davies as managing director, and had the plant producing boats by July 1972. That year was a break-even year. The boat was priced too low and, by the time they realized it and increased the price to $745, most of that year's production of 2,100 boats had been sold.

But profit, at that point, wasn't their chief concern. Potential competition was. The Laser's success was almost frightening, because Performance Sailcraft was in an odd position: they'd developed an innovative, popular product; but, unlike most manufacturers of innovative products, they had no protection. Any company in the world, if it chose, was free to manufacture a boat almost *exactly* like the Laser. "The cold hard fact," says Bruce, "is that if somebody had taken the Laser, just changed one or two small things and marketed it, there isn't a thing we could have done about it." As a matter of fact, at least two firms did exactly that.

The Laser's surest protection, Bruce realized very early, was the confidence and enthusiasm of the people who sailed her. They'd bought the boat for racing; so the company, long before it showed a profit, invested heavily in building an association of Laser owners, a class organization to organize races and set the rules of competition. They paid the salary for a full-time organizer for the class, who worked out of Performance Sailcraft's offices. They published a class newspaper and sponsored regattas. The first North American championships were held in Baltimore in October 1971, and it was an indication of the Laser's growing acceptance that 90 competitors showed up, including some of the continent's best small-boat sailors.

In the summer of 1972, Bruce represented Canada at the Olympics in Kiel, Germany, sailing a Star. But he took along a Laser and, once again, basked in the admiration the boat attracted from some of the world's best sailors. The response confirmed something he'd been groping towards instinctively: a conviction that the Laser could be sold all over the world. "I realized at Kiel," says Bruce, "that this thing needn't be just another small Canadian product, that it could be a truly *international* class. The summer of '72 really crystallized my thinking and Ward's." As soon as he and McKimm returned from Europe, they decided to attempt something that, in the world of international sailing, was totally unprecedented, totally audacious: they were going to try to get the Laser certified as an international class.

There are at least 300 classes of sailboats in the world — designs of every imaginable shape and size. But there are only 19 *international* classes: designs that have been so designated by the International Yacht Racing Union, an august and slow-moving organization of gentlemen sailors who are the world arbiters of international sailing competition. The IYRU sets the design criteria for each of these 19 classes, and any firm willing to meet these criteria is free to build an international boat, so long as it pays royalties to the IYRU. Working within the Union's design parameters, competing builders strive to devise faster boats in each class. That's what international competition is all about: a war of designers as much as sailors.

Performance Sailcraft's proposal was audacious and unprecedented because the firm wanted international status for a boat in which no design variations would be allowed; and because the firm proposed to remain the world's only builder. To the uninitiated, the concept still seems a bit staggering. "You mean," I asked Bruce, "that it's like CCM asking to be certified as the only firm in the world that can make hockey pucks?"

"Well, yes," he replied — "at least the only pucks that can be used in pro hockey."

126

To even suggest such a thing made Bruce feel as though he were back in dancing school. Most of his friends thought he'd flipped out. Why should the IYRU grant what amounts to a worldwide monopoly to a young company in Montreal? "Everyone thought we were absolutely mad. They didn't think we had a hope in hell of getting the thing through."

But there has been an eerie smoothness about every aspect of the Laser's development. Its design wasn't the product of endless, anguished months; it sprang almost full-grown from Bruce Kirby's scratchpad. Building the prototype was a silky process too; there were no production hitches, and it came out of its virgin mold as smoothly as a pancake from a well-buttered griddle. Even the company's development went smoothly. Performance Sailcraft once had a line of bank credit cancelled suddenly and awkwardly, but in the early years the firm didn't face the horrendous cash crises that are the daily burden of most Canadian entrepreneurs. And so, when Bruce and Kirby flew to London in November 1972, to make their pitch before the IYRU's Class Policy and Organization Committee, the same eerie smoothness asserted itself once again.

The meeting was held at the Royal Thames Yacht Club. The committee, which included King Constantine of Greece, represented the cream of international yachting. Bruce and Kirby had modest hopes. "At our first appearance we'd hoped to lay the groundwork for a successful pitch the following year," Bruce says. That seemed unlikely, but even the most skeptical conceded that the two Canadians were holding several strong cards. Not entirely by accident, they'd staged the first British Laser championships the day before at St. Mary's Reservoir, outside London. Sixty-five boats had entered, sailed by some of Britain's top sailors, an impressive showing whose import was not lost on the committee. Besides, for months there had been extremely favorable publicity appearing in yachting magazines on both sides of the Atlantic. Most important, at the moment when Kirby and Bruce stood up before those 20 nautical gentlemen, seated around the club's long board-room table, they had *numbers* behind them. Four thousand Lasers were being sailed and raced around the world. The following year, they were confident, there would be 10,000.

Bruce and Ward McKimm had prepared a lengthy written

brief for the meeting, and they were braced for a long and probing examination. Instead — and Bruce still shakes his head in wonderment when he recalls the moment — the motion went through in less than three minutes, with practically no discussion. Beppe Croce of Italy, the committee's chairman, made a few introductory remarks; the Laser, he said, could be the boat the IYRU had been waiting for: the ultimate one-design racer, the boat that would finally democratize the sport. King Constantine quietly raised his hand and moved that the Laser be granted provisional status as an international class. There was a show of hands, the vote was unanimous and — that was all. "I was sitting there, and I couldn't believe it," says Bruce. "It absolutely shattered us."

Before the vote, there had been some brief discussion of how unthinkable it would be for Performance Sailcraft to hold a monopoly on the manufacture of an international-class boat. Someone said the class rules would have to be changed to permit multiple manufacturers, and everyone nodded. But by the fall of the next year, at a meeting of the IYRU's Centreboard and Technical Committee, which also had to approve the decision, it had become clear that an effective monopoly was the only course available.

By this time, there were 10,000 Lasers in the water; the speedy little boat from Montreal had become the most exciting innovation in the world of sailing. Because the company had spent $40,000 subsidizing it, there was an active class organization in North America and Europe. And the way canny Ward McKimm had drafted the rules and constitution of the class, any proposed changes in the design of the boat, or in the rules governing the class, had to be approved by both the company and by 75 percent of the class association's membership. The IYRU was faced with a *fait accompli:* the fastest-growing class in the world. "The political reality was that the Union had to take a chance on us as we were, or forget about the whole thing. There was no way that 75 percent of the members were going to allow the IYRU to rewrite their constitution."

The Laser, the IYRU was beginning to realize, is probably the most *uniform* boat in the world. The class rules drafted by McKimm were the tightest for any class in the world. Every Laser centreboard, for instance, must be supplied by the builder, and no variation greater than five millimetres is allowed. Every Laser sail is made under Performance Sailcraft's supervision, and to rigid specifications. One of these specifications is the stretch characteristics of the cloth. In 1972 alone, Hans Fogh rejected 10,000 yards of Dacron cloth because it didn't meet those requirements. Even the size of the identifying letters on the sail are spelled out in the class rules: eight by 12 inches. When the IYRU dispatched its measurement specialist to Montreal to test the boat for uniformity, he discovered what company officials had known for years: that every Laser is virtually identical to every other Laser. The greatest discrepancy the expert was able to unearth was an occasional difference in weight; some hulls weighed as little as 125 pounds; others were nearly 135.

Finally, at its spring meeting in 1974, the IYRU voted to grant full international-class status to the Laser. By this time there were 15,000 boats in the water, and the Union, by agreement, was to receive $2 per boat — the kind of money that an organization with a small budget can scarcely afford to ignore.

Under the agreement between Performance Sailcraft and the IYRU, it wasn't *quite* a monopoly. The Union may license other manufacturers to build the boat, but only with Performance Sailcraft's approval. And Bruce wasn't about to grant approval until his company finished setting up its own global manufacturing operation. This wasn't greed. It was prudence. If manufacturing were dispersed into too many hands, there was an acute danger that variations might creep into the design — which would destroy the credibility of the one-design concept that is the real basis of the Laser's popularity. "Sure, it's an extremely strong position to be in," says Bruce, "but there's a fair responsibility that goes with it." One Union official, after international status was awarded, told Bruce and McKimm privately: "You two guys are on the line. If you do it right, this could be the greatest thing that's ever happened to sailing. But if you screw it up, it's going to be the biggest screw-up in the history of the sport."

Bruce and McKimm had no intention of screwing up. By 1975, they'd set up other plants in Brazil, Australia, New Zealand and Ireland, and opened a sales subsidiary in Japan. All Laser factories produce boats from molds shipped from Montreal, and all the production managers have spent a training period in Montreal. The sails, which are the easiest part of the boat to tinker with, and therefore the part requiring the strictest control, are made by Chesapeake Cutters in Annapolis, Maryland, a company jointly owned by Performance Sailcraft and Haarstick Sailmakers. The patterns are programmed into a computer, which operates an automatic sail-cutting machine that cuts the panels and joins them together by an ultrasonic heat-seal method. At that point, the design is "locked in," and the sails are shipped to authorized sailmakers in several countries for finishing. Performance Sailcraft, in other words, is manufacturing Lasers the way Coca-Cola manufactures Coke. There have been successful one-design boats before, but no one has ever executed the one-design concept so strictly.

That concept, as applied by Performance Sailcraft, is transforming the sport of sailing. The best way to see this is by attending a Laser regatta. At regattas for most classes, the atmosphere before a race carries undertones of tension and concern. Sailors anxiously tinker with their boat's rigging and fittings, hoping to extract some miniscule advantage. When they're not working on their own boats, they're checking out the competition's. At a Laser regatta, however, what the competitors mostly do before a race is quaff a few beers, while the boats sit unnoticed on the beach. There's nothing to inspect, nothing to tinker with; Laser competition takes place on the water, not on the drawing board.

The Laser's popularity has made Bruce the subject of rags-to-riches stories in the newspapers. He's even become accustomed to MBA students dropping around to interview him for their theses. All the callers assume that he, McKimm and André Julien must be incredibly canny; that they shrewdly spotted a vacuum in the marketplace and moved swiftly to fill it.

"That's bullshit," says Bruce. "We've never done a market survey, ever. The design was good, and what we did with the design was good. But the whole Laser story is just an extraordinary stroke of luck. The timing was absolute chance. If we'd come out with the boat two years earlier, it would have fallen flat on its ass. If we'd come out two years later, it would have been too late." They were lucky too, in their financing arrangements. Nearly all the expansion, all the development of the class organization, all the initial promotion, was financed by loans from banks and the four shareholders (although, in mid-1975, a Toronto venture-capital firm, Canadian Venture Capital Corp., bought 30 percent of the company for $500,000). And because the company is run by men who are known and respected wherever there are yacht clubs, their most effective advertising has been word of mouth among the kind of people they've been sailing with for years.

In that sense, Performance Sailcraft is still a hobby company, even though Bruce and McKimm now work at it full-time. But there was nothing casual about the work load that created the company, or the series of decisions that led to its worldwide growth. Something like the Laser can only happen, says Bruce, "if there are one or two individuals prepared to dump everything they've got into it. You just can't even *think* about salary, about your standard of living, about the rate of return, about your investment of time or anything else. If I hadn't been prepared to take a $16,000 cut in salary, the thing wouldn't have happened." Only entrepreneurs, it seems, understand that entrepreneurs aren't in it for the money.

8

RUSS BENSON'S
FRUSTRATING HUNT
FOR MONEY

It is great fun to play with Russ Benson's invention, which is a machine that squashes up garbage, any kind of garbage, more efficiently than any other machine yet devised. It is even more fun to watch Russ Benson play with his invention, because he gets such a kick out of it. He enjoys taking visitors down to his company's little workshop in North Vancouver where one of the prototypes is installed, and showing them what the thing will do. First he tosses one of those quart-sized pineapple juice cans into the hopper. There is a whir and a crunch, and the can drops out onto the floor below, now looking like an *objet trouvée* from a Manhattan art gallery.

"Okay," says Benson, "That was easy. Now let's try a phone book." He tosses in a battered copy of last year's Vancouver directory. The machine, whose guts consist mainly of a rotating shaft with a lot of teeth, plus some iron grillwork, then does something slightly surprising: it doesn't shred the phone book as you'd expect. Instead, it strains and whirs, and suddenly there is this enormous clang of metal slamming on metal, and the phone book drops down, still intact, on the floor. "See — there's no air in a phone book," says Benson. "There's nothing to squash, so it gives the book back to you."

Next, Benson throws in a block of wood the size of a small stump, and, once again, Benson's garbage-squashing machine demonstrates its devilish sophistication. The motor whirs, the axle revolves, the teeth grab the block of wood and press it against the

132

iron grating. The machine strains, but it obviously isn't strong enough to chew up this block of wood. So, automatically, the machine reverses itself. The axle turns backward, stops, then starts turning in the original direction. Once again the stump is pressed against the grating, once again the machine is stymied, once again it shifts into reverse. Thanks to some elaborate and highly original circuitry, the machine is programmed to make the attempt exactly six times, then quit. "You can throw anything into this thing," says Benson. "*Anything*. And if it can't handle it, it tells you so."

I am not an engineer, but even I can sense the brute elegance of Russ Benson's Rabco garbage compactor. Most compactors — including the ones you see (and, regrettably, hear) on garbage trucks — work on some kind of piston principle; they tamp the stuff down into its container. Some are extremely powerful and effective, but the principle is basically the same as a man stomping on a canful of garbage with his foot.

Benson's machine works on an entirely different principle, and the easiest way to explain how it works is to imagine a wringer washer. One roller has teeth on it — not just spikes sticking out, but a series of large, wing-like vanes. If you saw this roller all by itself, it would look something like a spiral staircase, with the steps fanning out in a helix pattern around a centre post. The other roller isn't really a roller at all, because it doesn't rotate. It looks more like the business end of a rake. The vanes on the first roller, as they rotate, pass through the spaces between the teeth on the second roller. As they do, anything that's been tossed into the machine and trapped by the rotating teeth gets squashed or ripped or chewed up before dropping out the bottom.

At the bottom, of course, you've got a container — and this brings up one of the more elegant aspects of Benson's brainchild. When the container is full, the top of the pile touches the wing-like blades of the roller. As more garbage is fed in and the axle keeps rotating, the garbage already in the container gets pumped down by the machine's rotating action, pretty much like a rolling pin squashing dough.

The principle is so elegant, the operation so efficient, that it only takes a three-horsepower electric motor to drive the thing. This power, transmitted through a belt and then a gearbox, makes the axle rotate slowly, but with enormous force.

If you throw in something too solid for the machine to squash — like the phone book — another Benson innovation comes into play. Instead of jamming the machine, the pressure of the indigestible phone book forces the rake-like assembly back away from the rotating roller, so the book can fall to the bottom, unsquashed. Then the rake-like assembly, which is on hinges, is slammed back into place by a powerful air-cushion spring. That's the metallic bang you heard.

When Benson demonstrated his machine at a trade show in Germany in 1971, it was obvious to that international community of men who are paid to worry about how to get rid of garbage that Russ Benson had indeed invented a better mousetrap. Inquiries and business offers came pouring in from Denmark, Germany, Sweden, Italy, the U.S., Britain — from practically every country, in fact, that is affluent enough to have a garbage problem.

And here, according to the conventional wisdom, the story should end happily: back-yard tinkerer builds better mousetrap; world beats path to door; inventor retires to clip coupons. In fact, Russ Benson's problems were only beginning. In the growth cycle of any company, the development of an acceptable product is only the first step in a long and painful process, a process that many companies fail to complete. For, once you've built a better mousetrap, you have to figure out a way to sell it. Even more crucially, you have to convince outside investors that your product has the potential for profit, and that you're the man to exploit that potential.

Russ Benson is a dogged and determined man. He built his machine by a painstaking process of trial and error. And he set out to raise money the same way. It was a frustrating and, in some ways, a humiliating process. As it turned out, he failed to raise much money from outside investors. But in the end he managed to finance the company's growth with revenues generated from sales. He's built a small and successful company, but he did it without the support of the Canadian financial community, a group Benson now believes to be conservative almost to the point of idiocy.

So this isn't just a treatise about a man who built a better mousetrap. It's a case history about all the things that can go wrong after the mousetrap is perfected — and about the cultural gulf that separates people who build mousetraps from people who raise the money to manufacture them.

Benson has iron-gray hair, a small moustache and an air of brisk authority. He is very much a self-made man, and isn't good at disguising his impatience with those who aren't. He is accustomed to giving orders and assuming that they'll be carried out. Some people he's worked with describe him as prickly. But there is also a broad streak of imagination and creativity in his makeup. At the University of British Columbia, he studied architecture and engineering. He liked the idea of architecture: "We were told that architecture is an expression of freedom, providing that what you design is structurally sound." And there was something about that combination of structure and creative anarchy that appealed to him.

But then, as a class exercise, he designed a church — a soaring, swooping structure with a parabolic roof — and his professor didn't like it. "It doesn't look like a church," is what the learned man said. Benson argued, and was awarded a zero for the assignment. Benson found this a disillusionment, so he promptly said the hell with it and quit architecture school. "I'm a rebel in many respects," he says. What he means, I suspect, is that he'll fight like hell when anyone tries to stop him from doing things his way. Most good inventors, and all good artists, are like that.

The next step for Russ Benson was a boring job in the drafting room at Thompson, Berwick, Pratt and Partners, a leading firm of Vancouver architects. He found it frustrating, and, almost as soon as he'd settled into the job, started looking for a way out of it. He found it one morning in 1949, when a salesman named Len Corcoran walked into the architects' offices, trying to interest the firm in a line of metal windows he was manufacturing. "I didn't want to be pushing a pencil for the rest of my life," says Benson, "so I joined Corcoran's firm as a salesman. This made it a two-man operation."

Ten years later, the operation had become the largest supplier of metal windows in Western Canada, doing $3 million worth of business a year and consuming a boxcar-load of sheet glass every week. Benson, by now entitled vice-president and general manager, spent much of his life on the road, flogging windows to architects and construction firms as far east as Toronto. The two men also devised, received patents for and began selling a novel system of metal curtain-wall cladding for high-rise office buildings, through a subsidiary company called Columbia Manufacturing Ltd.

"During this period," he says, "I developed a dandy set of ulcers. It was getting to be a frightful rat race. Everybody and his brother and their dog was getting into the metal-window business. So, partly on the advice of my doctor, after 12 years I sold out to Corcoran." For a man of Russ Benson's age, it wasn't a bad spot to be in. His former partner bought out his interest in the firm at the rate of $800 a month, and supplied him with a car besides. It wasn't Easy Street, but it did give Benson the leisure and the wherewithal to look around for his next deal.

Benson then borrowed $15,000 from the bank and bought into a firm called Almetco Manufacturing Co. Soon afterward, his former firm went bankrupt, paying its creditors five cents on the dollar, which meant that Benson no longer had the $800-a-month cushion. And soon after *that*, he sold his interest in Almetco because of disagreements with his partners. By this time, Benson had decided that he worked best on his own. And so in 1962 he formed his own company, R. A. Benson Co. Ltd., which acted as a manufacturers' agent, specializing in architectural products for hospitals and schools: anything from foldaway gymnasium seats to office partitions. "I knew all the architects," says Benson, "so it was pretty well natural for me. But I didn't want to go back into windows. That game's a dog's breakfast."

Operating as a husband-and-wife team, R. A. Benson Ltd. was quietly successful. "The idea was to have a nice quiet little business in Vancouver. But within 18 months I was doing business in Alberta and Winnipeg, and within three years we were selling right across the country. I sure as hell didn't plan it that way, but I was back traveling again." In its best year, the firm's sales were $400,000.

Keeping in touch with his customers, school and hospital administrators, is what finally led him into the wonderful world of garbage compaction. Benson frequently attended conventions and

136

trade shows, and over a period of years he noticed a major trend in the hospital-equipment industry: everything — hypodermic needles, scalpels, surgical gowns and gloves, you name it — was going disposable. Benson started wondering how hospitals proposed to get rid of all these hygienic throw-aways. "It was more morbid curiosity than anything else, so I started asking around. I asked the manufacturers of disposable items how you get rid of all this stuff. I asked the hospital administrators too. They all said, 'Well, you just throw the stuff away.' Nobody had any answers."

So Benson started looking at the various brands of garbage compactors, which were just then, around 1967, becoming a factor in the market. He was looking for a product to add to his line of hospital equipment, and the compactor he finally chose, made by a U.S. firm, seemed to be the best one on the market.

"But it didn't really work," says Benson. "It was a sort of oversized garburator that used a wet-pulp process to reduce the volume of garbage. But it wouldn't handle metal or glass, and it got plugged up by plastic. The product simply didn't perform the way the man said it would." Benson, by choice, didn't sell a single unit. Instead, armed with the knowledge that the best product on the market didn't work very well, he started doodling on scratch pads, looking for his own alternative.

In July 1968, somebody — he can't remember who — dropped into his office, and they got talking about the compaction problem. Benson started sketching solutions on the scratch pad on his desk. What he came up with, and later polished into detailed working drawings, was a device with four rollers. The first pair would crush the garbage, and the second pair would shred it. "It's hard to say where any idea germinates, but let me explain it this way: the problem was to crush everything up, right? Well, that reminded me of my mother's old clothes wringer. So I started thinking about counter-rotating drums, only with teeth on them."

So, now we approach one of the Moments of Truth in the entrepreneurial life cycle: the man had an idea, and he'd drawn a sketch of it. Most of us would leave it at that. But what made Benson decide to risk his own time and his own money turning that idea into a machine? The inventor himself can't answer that one, but there were a few factors operating in Benson's favor that prompted him to embark on the process that was to dominate his life for the next few years. For one thing, his hospital and school supply business was by now practically running itself, paying him a salary of $12,000 a year, and returning an annual profit of $15,000 or so besides. He wasn't exactly financially independent; but at least his firm gave him enough of a cushion to devote part of his time to the new idea, and to hire someone to help turn it into reality.

Besides, he'd helped develop new products before, back in his metal-window period with Corcoran. In the previous 15 years, Benson estimates, he'd been involved with the development of about a dozen new products. The innovation process wasn't a complete mystery to him. More to the point, he was a tinkerer and a dreamer, with a long history of fighting for the right to dream and tinker in *exactly* his own way.

And so he began. Benson incorporated a new company, named Benson Industries Ltd. and set up shop in a two-car garage on Keith Road in North Vancouver. He bought a set of small hand tools and some welding equipment, hired part-time mechanics on an hourly basis when he needed them, farmed out some of the early fabrication jobs to local machine shops, and started to tinker in earnest.

The original concept of two pairs of rollers was the first victim of the research. Benson, after building several prototypes and experimenting with rollers that turned at different speeds, simplified the concept to a two-roller device. Eventually, after experimenting with speeding one roller up and slowing the other down, he arrived at the one approach that worked: one toothed roller that revolved slowly, and another roller that didn't revolve at all. "It was one of those unusual situations where you start with something fairly large and complex," says Benson, "and come down to something small and simple."

This process of eliminating rollers, experimenting with different reduction-gear systems and various-sized motors took about six months. "We had celebrations and funerals constantly. We knew there had to be an answer to this problem. But there's no handbook. There's nothing you can refer to. You can't build on somebody else's experience, and you can't copy. So you go up many blind alleys." All of them cost money. By early 1969, Benson had spent several thousand dollars on his idea, and most of his free time. He'd come up with a design concept which, although it looked promising, was untested. He'd reached the stage where he needed more money to carry the thing further, and couldn't provide it out of his own savings.

That, fortuitously, was when someone told him about the federal government's Program for the Advancement of Industrial Technology (PAIT), and gave him the name of an official in the Department of Industry, Trade and Commerce who processed PAIT applications. Benson phoned the man in Ottawa. The official was coming to Vancouver, so the two men soon met. The ITC official liked what he saw and became, in effect, Benson's ally in Ottawa. Six months later, Benson Industries received approval of a PAIT grant of $28,000. A friend of Benson's, an insurance underwriter named Roger Latta, also helped. Through friends and clients, he and Benson raised about $78,000 "in dribs and drabs," selling shares in the private company at 50 cents each.

By this time, Benson needed more than a handyman to perfect the device. With the PAIT payments coming in every month, he was able to hire a millwright named Les Charlton, Dr. Rod Cameron as chief engineer, and an electronic expert named Nick Fletcher, who designed the sophisticated control system that enables the Rabco compactor to make so many decisions. By the autumn of 1970, the design team felt they had a machine that looked good enough for field tests. They installed the first unit in a new apartment complex. The machine sat at the bottom of the building's garbage chute, quietly chewing up, squashing or rejecting whatever was tossed down to it.

Except, of all things, panty hose. "It was the damnedest thing," says Benson. "That stuff, panty hose, has enormous tensile strength. It would wrap itself around and around the axle and simply jam the works. The machine couldn't move. So we put in some modifications. It's sort of a trade secret how we beat the problem, but it involves abrasive surfaces. We put some rough patches on the metal so it saws through the panty hose before it can gum up the works. Panty hose! Hell, there's no way you could foresee a problem like that. That's what field testing is *for* — to discover these problems and solve them before you put your product on the market."

By the end of 1970, Benson had several units operating in various sites around Vancouver, deliberately selected to provide experience in a range of potential uses: St. Paul's Hospital, a McDonald's hamburger emporium (where management found the machine was providing a better volume reduction than they'd been getting by burning their garbage), several more apartment blocks, the Vancouver Hotel. As a result of these initial experiences, Benson built additional modifications into later machines —harder steel and larger teeth, mainly. But the machine's users were uniformly enthusiastic. International recognition came soon afterward. The machine's unveiling at the trade show in Stuttgart was a critical triumph, but there were other accolades as well. George Trezek, an associate professor of engineering at the University of California, who specializes in waste-disposal problems, flew up from Berkeley to inspect the machine, and came away mightily enthused. Most of the compaction machines Dr. Trezek has inspected work on the "hammer-mill" principle, where the garbage is pounded down. The Rabco unit impressed him because it requires so little power; because it works so quietly (hammer-mill units, he says, operate "near the threshold of pain"); and because it's so safe. In 1973, the machine won a "best engineering" award from the American Iron and Steel Institute. The award is presented for "the imaginative use of steel in a structure, product or art form," and, in manufacturing circles, it's equivalent to a Pulitzer Prize.

At this point, the focus of our story shifts abruptly. From here on in, Russ Benson's problems became financial rather than technological. He knew his product was a winner, so now he had to embark on a search that was totally alien to his experience: a hunt for money, the kind of money you need to transform what still was, after all, not much more than a workshop in a two-car garage into the kind of company whose name and product is recognized all over the world — a company with brochures and head offices and marketing experts and vice-presidents and all the rest. All his life, Benson had been dealing with the foot soldiers of capitalism: salesmen, product managers, purchasing agents, production men — always people whose livelihoods depended on an intimate relationship with things, and the way those things behaved for their customers.

Now, as he began his search for capital, he encountered a new and almost frightening breed: soft-spoken men in pin-striped suits who didn't know a grommet from a valve, but who spent their lives evaluating men who did; men who somehow had access to large pools of other people's savings, and were skilled at choosing situations where that money was most likely to grow. These people were mostly intelligent and deferential and interested. But somehow they never seemed to get on the same wavelength with Russ Benson. There is a broad cultural gap between men who manage things and men who manage money. From the moment he started looking for money, Russ Benson came up against this gap, and he never quite succeeded in crossing it.

There are probably more intriguing ideas chasing money in Vancouver than any city of a million or so has any right to expect. This is simply because a great many technological entrepreneurs, like anyone else in his right mind, prefer to live in Vancouver. "The nature of the place attracts these kinds of people," says a seasoned official of the provincial Department of Industrial Development, Trade and Commerce, who has looked closely at many of these young B.C. companies. "Look at it this way: Let's say you're some guy from Control Data or IBM, you're living in some place like Cleveland or Minneapolis, you're about 35, you've got $100,000 or so, and you've got this itch to start your own company. Well, you're in the position where you can set that company up almost anywhere. So you try it here — where you can sail and swim and ski. It's all here: good universities, because we're the economic shadow of California, lots of input, lots of intellectual stimulation. Plus the climate, eh? So this is where you set up your company. Hell, you can always fly back to Cleveland three days a month to consult, right?"

And so, in almost any season in Vancouver, you hear about intriguing new companies based on some idea that will revolutionize an industry, if only they can get the financing. There's a company growing tomatoes without any soil; a company building and selling small research submarines; a company that's trained a computer to scan aerial photographs and correct their distortions; a company making plastic tire chains; a company making tiny crystal chips, each the size of a flake of oregano, which function as FM radio transmitters. And so on.

To get money for such ventures, you can either persuade individual investors to gamble their money; or, if the company has a record of earnings, float a public stock issue; or, if your company is at an earlier stage of development, attempt to persuade a venture-capital firm to invest; or look for a merger with a larger firm — or a judicious combination of all of the above. Russ Benson, who cheerfully admits he knew nothing about raising money, tried all these approaches, and got nowhere. The way he conducted his search, and the responses he received from the financial community, provide an instructive glimpse into how and why young companies grow, and often fail to grow, in this country.

Benson's first stop was at Pemberton Securities, a long-established Vancouver brokerage house which, in a market dominated by mining stocks, has underwritten several successful industrial issues. "I chose Pemberton's because they were just the right size, and well connected across the country," says Benson. "I knew it was probably too early for a public offering, but I went there with the idea that sooner or later we'd have to have public money."

Pemberton quickly agreed that, yes, it was much too early to be thinking about a public stock issue. "We decided it was a venture-capital situation," says Pemberton's vice-president, Dick Thompson, who worked with Benson on the deal, "and we were hoping to find some private money and make a three-percent commission. Our experience in underwriting junior industrials is that the company should have a reasonable level of earnings so it can withstand a bad year. But, hell, Russ was just getting his prototypes off the ground. There was no reasonable level of earnings — in fact, there was every possibility of the company continuing to show a loss."

During a bull market, at a time when stocks are rising merrily and investors are willing to buy anything that sounds sexy, Benson might have had no trouble getting a public underwriting. Only a few years earlier, investors on the Vancouver Stock Exchange had cheerfully gambled millions of dollars on companies whose products and prospects, putting it charitably, were a lot less promising than Russ Benson's. But this was 1971, not 1968, and investors were buying industrial stocks on the basis of what the companies were earning, not what they hoped to earn.

Still hoping to interest some private investor, Pemberton went to work investigating Benson's product and its prospects. Dick Thompson talked to various companies in the anti-pollution field, trying to develop a feel for the industry. Will garbage disposal really be big business in the next 10 years? And if so, what kind of products are likely to be in greatest demand? Thompson concluded, as many analysts have done before and since, that a large new market was developing, and that Benson's compactor seemed like the right product at the right time.

The first step in the hunt for money was to contact other manufacturing companies that might be interested either in a joint venture, or in buying out Benson Industries and manufacturing the Rabco compactor themselves. There were preliminary discussions with several firms, including subsidiaries of Hawker Siddeley and Bow Valley Industries. In all, there were half a dozen such approaches, but none of them led anywhere.

The next step was to contact the venture-capital companies, those exotic corporate entities that make a living by investing in small companies, in the hopes that they'll become big ones. Venture capital is a relatively new discipline in Canada; there are only about 50 firms in the whole country that describe themselves with this label, and most of them started in the late 1960s. There is an exquisite and particular art involved in guessing which young companies are worth supporting and which aren't. To a man, venture capitalists avow that they always invest in "people, not products." What they're gambling on isn't the product itself, but the abilities of the man who proposes to bring that product to market. There's another axiom in the venture-capital business too; the man who invents a gizmo and the man who creates the International Gizmo Corp., the big-league production and marketing organization, are hardly ever the same people.

And that is why, when Dick Thompson of Pemberton took Benson's deal to the Vancouver office of Canadian Enterprise Development Corp., one of the country's largest — and, some say, one of the stodgiest — venture-capital firms, it was not the Rabco compactor that was being judged, so much as it was Russ Benson himself.

CEDC is a consortium of some of the nation's largest banks, insurance and trust companies who, in 1962, put together a pool of about $11 million and hired small teams of analysts to choose young companies which, with an infusion of start-up capital, might become large companies. CEDC is like any other venture firm; although it traffics in the very essence of risk, it doesn't gamble blind. Nothing is so cautious as a million dollars, so a deal must look right and smell *very* right before a firm like CEDC parts with its money.

At first the deal smelled very right indeed. A CEDC man — let's call him John Smith — met with Benson and Dean Alexander of Pemberton on March 10, 1971. He spent the next day poking around in the various basements where Rabco compactors were installed, and talking to the people who used the equipment. He also talked money with Russ Benson, who wanted CEDC to buy 125,000 shares at $2 per share. A few days later, Smith wrote a memo for internal circulation, summarizing everything he knew and felt about the deal. It was a promising product, Smith wrote, and Benson was an experienced and successful businessman. Still, the deal seemed a little rich; and Smith felt he'd like to see Benson with more of a financial stake in the venture.

The negotiations simmered for several months. CEDC suggested to Benson that $2 a share was a bit steep, and Benson — who'd sold shares to private investors for as little as 50 cents, and as much as $2 — agreed.

By mid-June, Benson and CEDC had reached the stage of detailed negotiating. CEDC suggested putting about $100,000 into the company through a debenture note. If converted into equity, CEDC officials say, this would have been equivalent to buying 125,000 shares at $1.50 each. This was only an exploratory suggestion, however. To become a formal offer, it would first have had to be approved by CEDC's board of directors. And it never got that far, because Benson and *his* board were cool to the terms. They felt it involved yielding too much control in return for too little money. The whole thing was very tentative, but it was the closest Benson and CEDC ever came to a deal.

CEDC still felt the company had excellent potential, and in a memo written in August, Smith listed the courses he thought CEDC could take to get Benson Industries off the ground. The first option, which Benson had already rejected, was for CEDC to find an acceptable president for the company, then invest in it. Another course would be to find a company to buy out Benson Industries, then invest in that other company. Another option would be to find a company that could, in effect, act as a subcontractor for marketing the product. In all these scenarios, it was assumed that Benson would become chairman of the board, with special responsibility for development of new products — the task for which, in Smith's view, Benson was best fitted — while a new man would actually run the company. This could be achieved either by hiring a man directly, or by arranging a corporate marriage.

CEDC had concluded, as had several other people who'd looked at the company, that Benson wasn't the best man to run it during its selling phase. He'd done a superb job developing the product. But he knew nothing about international marketing, and the Rabco compactor was a product that could be sold all over the world. (Since that time, however, Benson has learned plenty about international marketing; he's negotiated licensing agreements in half a dozen countries.)

By autumn, negotiations between Benson and CEDC were at a standstill. In October, at Benson's request, CEDC sent back all the documents it had used in its investigation of the company. And that was the end of the relationship. Benson, still plugging, then went back to Pemberton, the firm that had put him in touch with CEDC in the first place.

Pemberton tried some more, and so did Benson. He contacted Charterhouse Canada Ltd., a Toronto-based venture-capital firm. He flew to Toronto to outline the deal. Charterhouse was impressed with the product, but not with the management. A man from First National City Bank flew from Toronto to have a look; his conclusions were similar. Benson and Thompson also contacted Mike Brown of Brown, Farris and Jefferson, a Vancouver-based venture-capital firm, which was later to become one of the affiliated companies of the Canada Development Corp. Brown interested a Toronto company, Murritt Photofax, in the deal. But Murritt ran into problems of its own, and lost interest in a deal with Benson.

Benson tried other brokerage houses too, but the answer was always the same: you can't go public until you've got an earnings record; and you'll never get an earnings record until you hire some good marketing people and build a sales organization.

"But how in hell can you build a sales organization without the money to hire them?" says Benson. After more than a year of grubbing around for money, he had become an embittered expert on the deficiencies of capital markets in general, and of Vancouver financial institutions in particular. "It's so frustrating," he says. "I stick my neck out a country mile to promote something — sure, I hope to make a lot of money out of it — but I think it's reasonable to expect support from your neighbors.

"I tell you, it's a sad situation. There are so many ideas in this town, so many things developing. There has to be *some* way of helping."

But Benson is a determined man. Late in 1972, after a solid year of fruitless money-grubbing, he was still plugging. And finally he embarked on a course which, in financial circles, is usually regarded as an act of dogged, desperate courage: he floated an issue of Benson Industries stock, 200,000 shares at $2.50 each, without an underwriter.

The Benson stock was sold on a "best efforts" basis — which means, in effect, that your underwriter is so cool on your deal that, instead of buying your stock and reselling it to the public, he undertakes to sell it only on consignment. For the broker there is no risk and no commitment; only a lukewarm undertaking to do the best he can. C. M. Oliver was the reluctant brokerage house in this case; but it didn't want its name on the prospectus and, months after the issue came out, much less than one-quarter of the 200,000 shares had been sold, and most of that by a single energetic salesman.

Still, the issue did put about $60,000 into Benson's treasury, which was enough to ensure the company's survival until Benson figured out his next move.

Mostly, this consisted of selling Rabco units in British Columbia and Alberta, and exploring deals with overseas firms that were anxious to manufacture the machine abroad, under license. Benson received visitors from as far away as Japan and Sweden, and with some he signed agreements that gave Benson Industries a royalty on each machine manufactured and sold abroad. For those manufactured at home, he worked out subcontracting deals with several local companies; they'd build the components, and Benson Industries would do the final assembly in its North Vancouver headquarters. All of the electronic controls, however, would be built in North Vancouver and shipped to the foreign licensees.

In August 1973, there was a final episode in Russ Benson's long and fruitless flirtation with the financial community. Blyth Eastman Dillon & Co., a large U.S. investment house with a branch in Vancouver, came to Benson with a proposition. It had been looking at the garbage compaction market, and had concluded that Benson's machine was the best available. For a fee, the U.S. firm wanted to arrange further financing for Benson Industries. If it were successful, it might mean that Russ Benson would lose control of his company; but it would also mean that Benson Industries might achieve its full growth potential.

Joseph Reimann, the Blyth Eastman analyst who approached Benson, had already sketched out a growth scenario in his mind. "There are two things missing in Benson Industries as we see it. One is financing; the company's been chronically under-financed. The other is a lack of the kind of management that can take the company from its present early development stage to the major company stage. They've done a good job on development. Now the thing has to change pace — it has to be marketed aggressively, and from a strong financial base.

"We want to develop his company in two steps. In the first step, control of the company will pass into the hands of a small group or a few individual investors, with the financial strength to carry it for the next two years. During this time, an active effort will be made to expand the market for the product, within certain limits. At the end of two or three years, you'll have a well-financed company that's developed sufficient sales to be operating in the black.

"At that point, we feel the company should be sold to a much larger concern — somebody like Carrier Corp. or American Standard, a big firm with a large sales force and manufacturing capacity.

"The trouble with Russ is that he's not the type of individual who's capable of negotiating the financing of his company. This is something we see quite often — the transition from a small to a big business makes different calls on the management of a company. It requires different skills. It takes a different kind of person. Asking the same man to handle both stages of a company's growth is like saying that a guy brought up to play the violin should play the trombone. It's unfair."

Blyth Eastman's fee for bringing the company to maturity, with somebody else managing and controlling it, would have been five percent of whatever capital the investment firm succeeded in raising. Initially, it was looking for a private placement of about $1 million. The agreement signed with Benson gave the firm six months to find it. It wasn't successful. The agreement expired early in 1974, and Russ Benson was back where he started — the proprietor of a small company with a good product, but lacking the capital to expand beyond that.

For Benson, the affair with Blyth Eastman was another demonstration of the timidity of Canadian investors. He'd been willing to step aside; that was one of the stipulations of the Blyth Eastman agreement. But, even then, they were unable to find any investors.

By 1975, Benson had managed to build his company into a profitable operation. Sales in both the 1973 and 1974 fiscal years were in the $300,000 range, and the company in 1974 was able to repay its PAIT loan and show a $20,000 profit besides. Without a shred of support from the Canadian financial community, Benson had created a small success.

What he'd built wasn't nearly so grandiose as what the financial experts had envisioned. They'd explored mergers, joint ventures, outright sales, private placements — all sorts of routes that would have put hundreds of thousands of dollars into Benson's treasury, and made the company an important west-coast manufacturer. Instead, most Rabco units ended up being built abroad. Jobs that might have gone to Canadians went instead to Swedish and Australian and Japanese workers.

And the moral of it all? A venture capitalist would tell you that the moral is that self-made innovators like Russ Benson should step aside, once a product is developed, and let professional managers build the company from there.

148

But Benson was perfectly willing to do so — but even then, no Canadian institution was willing to take a chance on what they all conceded too be a world-beating product. One Industry, Trade and Commerce official who's followed the company's progress almost from the start, and who helped make several introductions to potential investors, says: "Some people think Russ is like a little bantam rooster — cocky as hell. Sure, some of his human skills haven't been honed as finely as they might be. But who's perfect? I think Russ has been very badly served by the venture-capital community. He's been a victim — a chronic victim in some cases."

Footnote: In the spring of 1975, someone finally decided to take a chance on Benson Industries. Needless to say, it wasn't a private financial institution. It was the federally sponsored Industrial Development Bank. In May, it agreed to make a substantial loan to the company and also bought a small amount of stock. It is extremely unusual for the IDB to take equity positions in anything. It did so in this case because Benson Industries, which farms out most of its manufacturing to subcontractors, has few assets it could pledge as security. The stock purchase, says one IDB official, "is a sweetener — it eases the pain of having no security. It was a way of getting into a venture that otherwise might not have had a chance to expand."

Benson had plenty of ideas for expansion. He wanted to develop a new version of the Rabco compactor that would fit on board a garbage truck. He'd also found that a larger, more powerful version of the compactor is capable of chewing up the contents of a garbage dump and spewing out clean landfill at the other end. He had plans. They weren't glamorous, but they were realizable. He'd proven that it could be done — even if he had to do it virtually alone.

9

THE LEGACY OF
JOSEPH-ARMAND BOMBARDIER

He had always been a perfectionist, a nail biter, a worrier, a man who tried to impose his notions of order on everything that touched him. And now, lying in a hospital bed in Sherbrooke, Quebec, with tubes feeding and draining his wasting body, knowing he had only a few weeks left, he conferred with his lawyer, who came daily to visit, and tried to tidy up the housekeeping details of the world he knew he'd soon be leaving.

Months earlier, even before the doctors told him he had cancer, Joseph-Armand Bombardier had begun straightening out his affairs. For estate-tax purposes, he'd bought his two brothers' shares in the business he'd founded as L'Auto-Neige Bombardier Ltée, the company that manufactured the strange-looking tracked vehicle he'd invented for personal travel over ice and snow. And he'd brought his son-in-law, a young chartered accountant named Laurent Beaudoin, into the business to add strength to the management team that would succeed him.

And now it was February, the deep night of a Quebec winter, a time of slate-gray skies and land the color of ice. Joseph-Armand had spent Christmas at home in Valcourt, the tiny village in Quebec's Eastern Townships where Bombardiers had lived since the 1840s. But now, after two serious operations, word of his illness had spread through the county and beyond. There were many messages, but few visitors: his wife and brothers and children, his business associates, a few old friends, a few favored priests. The priests had prepared for his arrival in the next world.

But it was his two advisors, accountant Jean-Paul Gagnon and lawyer Charles Leblanc, who ministered to his departure from this one.

Charles Leblanc came to Joseph-Armand's bedside almost every day for a month. The dying man's business had been his life. And so, in discussing the arrangements for its transfer to his heirs, an odd intimacy sprang up between them.

In discussing the future of a business, how could a man avoid revealing his feelings about the children who would inherit it? Joseph-Armand, through those dark February afternoons, spoke of his children's strengths and weaknesses. And he realized his paternal responsibility for both. If I hadn't been such a strong-willed man, he said one day to Leblanc, perhaps they would have turned out differently. He'd signed his will, he'd signed the documents creating a holding company for all his assets — even then, in 1964, they were worth several million dollars — he'd even signed the papers to establish a charitable foundation. Only one thing remained: he wanted to leave his children a *testament moral,* a father's parting words to the heirs who must continue his work. He asked Charles Leblanc to draft it, for Joseph-Armand was not skilled with words.

"Mes chers enfants," the testament began. "Two weeks ago, I learned that medical science can do nothing further for me. At my age I thought I could still do much for you, for my business and for my fellow citizens; but the end is in sight, and I place myself completely in the hands of my Creator. I thank him for having given me the faith necessary to pass this test . . . Within the limitations that God gave me, I have tried to raise you in the respect of His name, and to make of you men and dutiful women. I believe I have succeeded in this, and I ask you to continue to respect your mother as you have always respected her. Perhaps I have been brusque with you on some occasions. I realize that now; but I always wanted to do what I considered to be best for you . . ."

The language was austere and remote, like the man for whom it was written. But tears rolled down the lawyer's cheeks as he read this final document to the dying man, and Joseph-Armand was weeping too. He seized Leblanc's hand, and held it tightly as the lawyer read aloud: "It is my greatest desire that this inheritance be a source of unity rather than discord between you, or be-

151

tween you and your mother." The testament cautioned against *petites frictions* which, if not carefully managed, might degenerate into serious family disputes. To keep the company strong, and within the family, Joseph-Armand suggested that they create a board of directors consisting of five family members who were actively engaged in the business, plus two outsiders — one a specialist in finance and administration, another experienced in law and corporate procedure. The testament also cautioned against "dispersing your efforts in individual enterprises" and added: "Never forget that our company saw the light of day in a small garage in Valcourt, and it was the people of our village and the surrounding areas who always helped me make it what it is today. Always be humane in your relations with your employees." When he was finished reading, Leblanc asked his client if he wished to make any changes. Joseph-Armand, still weeping, signed it then and there.

Eleven days later, on February 16, he died. Leblanc had seen him in the morning, and Joseph-Armand was in an almost jovial mood. He was still being fed intravenously, and he pointed to a bandage he'd fastened in an odd way around the plastic tube, which was connected to a bottle of nutrient. "Charles," said Joseph-Armand, "how many people do you suppose had operations in this hospital today? How many in Sherbrooke? How many in *Canada*? And do you know what that bandage is? It's a regulator I invented. I'm supposed to get 10 drops a minute. Now — count the drops!"

Leblanc looked at his watch and counted. Sure enough: as the second hand swept around, he watched 10 drops of fluid course through the transparent tube. "If I'd known he was going to die that night, maybe I'd have asked for more details. Maybe he was kidding me — I don't know. But the point is: the day that man died, he was still inventing things."

Joseph-Armand spent most of his last afternoon with Helmut Rothe, an engineer whose firm in Austria supplied the two-cycle motors that powered a recent Bombardier development called the Ski-Doo. Rothe spoke no French and Joseph-Armand spoke no German. But they communicated happily for hours, with pencil and pad, discussing designs for a modified engine. It had been a good day. But the end came that night. There were two funeral

152

services in the old church next door to the Bombardier house on Valcourt's main street: one for the village, which hundreds attended; and a later service for family and close friends.

The snowmobile industry is the automobile industry in microcosm. The development of both machines brought a new piece of personal technology into the lives of hundreds of thousands of people. Both machines were revolutionary in the sense that they upset prevailing social patterns, changing landscapes and lifestyles, environments and economies. Both machines were the products of inspired tinkerers whose roots lay in the countryside. Henry Ford's Model T, the first car that almost anybody could afford, was a liberating influence in rural America; it ended the physical isolation that had been the dominant condition of North American life since the continent was settled.

The snowmobile's effect has been roughly the same wherever in the world the winters are harsh. Joseph-Armand Bombardier, according to local legend, became interested in tracked vehicles after one of his sons almost died of appendicitis one winter. Even then, as late as the 1930s, doctors made house calls on horse-drawn sleights, and rura villages like Valcourt, as soon as winter closed the roads, became almost as isolated and self-contained as the farms of the 19th century.

Bombardier, contrary to the legend which the company has carefully nurtured since his death, did not precisely invent the snowmobile. Inventors have been tinkering with the problem since the introduction of the automobile. In 1896, three brothers from Crested Butte, Colorado, received a U.S. patent for a "new and improved power-sled . . . which may be driven over the snow or ice with sufficient power to haul a load after it or upon it, which has easy means of steering it, which is constructed in such a way that it is not likely to slew, which has its driving mechanism adjustable to suit varying depths and conditions of snow." And in 1906, a doctor managed to get from Quebec City to Boston in mid-winter, aboard a tracked vehicle of his own design.

But Bombardier was the Henry Ford of the snowmobile, and Valcourt was his Dearborn. Born in 1907, the eldest of eight chil-

153

dren, he was an inventor from early childhood; the company's museum at Valcourt contains some of his youthful efforts — a toy boat with a clockwork motor, and a welding torch fashioned from a gasoline can and an old bicycle pump. He built his first snow vehicle when he was 15, using parts scrounged from his father's barn, and the motor from an old Model T Ford. The propeller-driven sled moved, but it was horrendously dangerous; Bombardier *père* ordered it dismantled on the spot.

Joseph-Armand never strayed far from Valcourt, where the first Bombardiers settled in 1842, or from his father's commands. He spent a brief period at a seminary in Sherbrooke, but never completed his course. He spent two and a half years in Montreal, working as a mechanic by day and studying mechanical and electrical engineering at night. In 1926, at his father's insistence, he returned to Valcourt. He was 19, and it was time to make a living. His father bought him a garage.

And that's where he remained for the next 10 years, repairing farm machinery and cars for a living, and tinkering with tracked vehicles the rest of the time. Once again, the parallels with the auto industry's beginnings are apparent; Bombardier simply built something to see how it worked and, when it failed to perform as he'd hoped, built something else. The products of these researches are on display today in the Bombardier Museum in Valcourt, each prototype vehicle embodying different technical approaches to the same problem. In a Model T which he adapted for snow travel in 1927, for instance, he added an extra set of rear wheels, and wrapped steel belt around them, to form a half-track tin lizzie. In a later version (1931), he'd replaced the steel belt, which was cumbersome and unreliable, with rubber tracks and added small wheels to the track assembly, like a tank. In 1932 and 1933, he built two other models that were driven by a propeller, powered by a Model T engine, with four runners instead of wheels, and a wooden body that looked more like an airplane's than a car's.

By 1934, he was back to tracks again. The latest prototype had an aerodynamic wooden body and half-tracks. But the major breakthrough was in 1935, when Bombardier built a prototype with a rubber-covered metal sprocket wheel, whose cogs fitted into slots on the rubber tracks, which were reinforced with steel rods. This approach worked better than anything he'd tried in the past 10 years, so he improved on it. In 1936, he built three or four such machines, with improved suspensions and a larger seating capacity. He even sold several of them, and took out a patent on the track, suspension and sprocket.

That same year, Bombardier developed his first commercial success: the seven-passenger B7. It used the sprocket-and-rubber-track system he'd patented, and it had a sheet-metal body which, viewed from the side, looked roughly like a Volkswagen. He built and sold more than two dozen of them for about $1,700 each and, the following winter, equipped them with more powerful engines and sold 100 more. He also started calling his garage L'Auto-Neige Bombardier.

The B7 quickly became part of the folklore of rural Quebec, and so did its inventor. The B7s were reliable, they were reason-comfortable (although unheated), they went anywhere, and they could carry a large payload of passengers or freight. Doctors bought them, and milkmen, and missionaries and rural telephone companies, and school boards and salesmen. In Bombardier's youth, and even up to the 1930s, it had taken a full day and three teams of horses to get the mail across 18 frozen miles from Water-loo — the nearest town of any size — to Valcourt. Equipped with a snowmobile, one of Bombardier's boyhood friends, a Valcourt restaurant-owner named Wilfrid Charbonneau, secured a mail delivery contract and, within a few years, was running three B7s around the clock, and covering the same distance in less than an hour.

As deliveries speeded up, so did the pace of life. Villages that had slumbered beneath the snow for six or seven months of the year suddenly became accessible to their neighbors, and to the outside world. "Life was wonderful then," Charbonneau recently recalled. "Mr. Bombardier's snowmobile revolutionized winter transportation, and life in winter in Quebec's villages. It became just as eventful as in summer." By the 1940s, the B7 was a recog-nized fixture of Quebec village life. Countless babies were deliv-ered by doctors who made their house calls in B7s. One or two babies were even born in B7s. And one or two at least, you might surmise, were conceived in B7s; the later models were roomy and equipped with efficient heaters.

The B7's success made Joseph-Armand Bombardier a man of substance in his own village, but it never succeeded in turning him into an administrator. Until 1941, when a rush of war contracts forced him to build larger quarters a few doors down the street from his home, he continued to work out of the garage where he'd begun in 1926. He had a roll-top desk in a cluttered office off the machine-shop floor, the kind of place where friends dropped in to pass the time of day. But he spent most of his days on the shop floor, endlessly tinkering with modifications to the machines that were about to make him rich.

"He was a perfectionist," recalls one visitor to that office. "He had to do everything himself — always out there, without a tie, working with the mechanics. I remember once, I was in there to talk some business, and they were adding a small cement floor to one corner of the shop. The old man dropped everything, and spent half an hour telling the guy who was laying the floor exactly how the concrete should be brushed — telling the contractor, in other words, how to do his job." He was good company when he wasn't working, which was seldom. The rest of the time, he was brooding, stubborn and hard to please, with a restless drive that sometimes would impel him to arise from a sleepless bed at four in the morning, get dressed and walk down the street to his shop, where he'd bore away at some technical problem until dawn. He was a chain-smoker and his nails were bitten short. After he quit smoking, he developed the nervous habit of tearing up an unlit cigarette and putting the shreds of tobacco in his mouth.

In 1940, Bombardier perfected the B12, a 12-passenger improvement on the B7, with an egg-shaped metal body, four portholes on each side, and an improved, full-track version of his patented sprocket-and-rubber-tread system. Defense authorities in Ottawa showed interest. Between 1942 and 1948, now installed in a new three-story building, L'Auto-Neige Bombardier sold 150 of them. He built troop-carrying versions for use in Norway, armored versions for the Canadian Army, and a stripped-down model designed for hauling pulpwood out of snow-bound forests.

By the end of the war, Bombardier Ltée was no longer a hole-in-the-wall operation. The new building on Rue St. Joseph, which had begun as a fair-sized machine shop, had been enlarged to the point where it looked like a genuine factory. And as the auto-

156

mobile industry discovered in the postwar years, Bombardier found he could sell as many vehicles as he could make. In the winter of 1945-46 alone, he sold between 200 and 300 of the B12s, and another 700 the year after that. Potential customers were trekking in to Valcourt from all parts of the world. Some wanted B12s. Others wanted Bombardier to build special versions for particular purposes — logging, oil exploration, travel on muskeg. By the mid-1950s, Bombardier's snow vehicles had become one of the few Canadian products to achieve a worldwide reputation. They were in use in the oil fields of northern Alberta, in forests from B.C. to Minnesota, in rural areas across the North American snow belt in the Arctic — wherever there was snow on the ground and work to be done.

Bombardier Ltée, by the late 1950s, had become one of Quebec's leading industries, the most impressive — in fact, almost the *only* – example of *Québecois* enterprise Making It Big. The company was still tightly controlled by Joseph-Armand. Two of his brothers worked with him, and had been given minority share positions, as had his purchasing agent and his secretary. In 1947, he'd bought a small plant in the village of Kingsbury, about 10 miles from Valcourt, and expanded it into a large factory in its own right, which manufactured the rubber treads for all Bombardier vehicles. His company was earning close to $1 million a year after taxes. There was no debt, and the cash simply kept piling up in the bank. The company now employed about 500 — virtually Valcourt's only industry — and its founder was the village's godfather. "The local council wouldn't so much as install a streetlight without consulting him," says one of his associates.

All through the 1950s, Joseph-Armand had been thinking of producing a small, personal tracked vehicle: something light and cheap, capable of carrying one or two passengers. He envisioned a modest but profitable sale to trappers and game wardens, a machine that would compete with dog teams in the Canadian north. The concept was scarcely new. In 1925, an inventor from Norway, Maine, named Charles H. Young had patented a "motor-driven sled" — not much more than a toboggan, really, with a motor mounted at the back end, and a single endless belt underneath the engine. Another American inventor, Carl Eliason of Sayner, Wisconsin, received a patent for a more sophisticated motorized toboggan in 1927. It was powered by a Johnson outboard motor, with a radiator adapted from a Model T, and Eliason sold about 40 of them, for $360 each, over the next five years.

In the 1930s, Eliason sold out to a company called Four Wheel Drive Corp., which manufactured the Eliason motor toboggan in Clintonville, Wisconsin, from 1939 to 1946, and then transferred production to its Canadian subsidiary in Kitchener, Ontario. FWD's Canadian engineers redesigned the product, putting the engine at the back instead of the front, and sold about 1,000 of them, many to governments for northern survey work. Except for the rear-mounted engine, it looked remarkably like the snowmobile of today. But in 1963, in a decision that must make FWD's management shudder every time they think of it, they discontinued production. "We'd moved into a new building, and the volume of our truck business was too great," recalls Clare Schnarr, FWD's general manager in Canada. "Motor toboggans were just a sideline with us. I wish we'd known then what we know now." One is tempted to speculate on what might have happened if FWD hadn't been the subsidiary of a U.S. company. Would it, instead of Bombardier, be the industry's giant today?

Back in Valcourt, Joseph-Armand was unconcerned by the prospect of competition from Kitchener or anywhere else. In 1957, he began testing his first prototype snowmobile — a bathtub-sized wooden box, mounted on the Bombardier sprocket-and-belt assembly, with skis at the front. In the spring of 1959, as the snow melted in Valcourt, he took his prototype to northern Ontario, where an old friend, Father Maurice Ouimet, had a mission at Lansdowne House, ministering to Eskimos and Indians in a vast wilderness area near James Bay. Father Ouimet became the world's first owner of a Ski-Doo, the brand name Bombardier had dreamed up for his new product. With the Ski-Doo, the priest found it took three hours to cover distances which, with a dog team, had often taken him three days and three nights.

That same year, Bombardier began manufacturing Ski-Doos, sold about 225 at $1,000 each, and discovered something curious: many of his customers didn't *need* a Ski-Doo; they were buying them, and driving them, mainly for fun. Anybody who's driven one can readily understand why, You feel a boyish, almost animal sense of freedom when you realize that the thing can go practically anywhere — shooting up snowbanks and down the other side, across roads and frozen lakes, anywhere an animal can go, almost. And because you're so close to the ground, and in such intimate, open contact with the wind and weather, it's hard to treat the Ski-Doo as simply an appliance for getting through the snow; the machine becomes an extension of your body and your senses — even of your fantasies. Trail motorcycles can give you this same sense of slightly anarchistic mobility. But in Canada a motorcycle is useless about half the year. The Ski-Doo's basic appeal was that, for the other half of the year, it enabled Everyman to venture, aboard an internal-combustion machine, into places where Everyman hadn't been able to venture before. Clearly, the snowmobile was an idea whose time had come.

A lot of people wished it hadn't. The popularity of the snowmobile coincided with an increasing ecological concern. Many viewed the new machine in about the same way they would a squadron of Harley-Davidsons invading a wildlife reserve. The same debate occurs with the introduction of every technical innovation whose effects are highly visible, from the automobile to television to the electric toothbrush. Any such innovation, sooner or later, is bound to be judged environmentally disastrous, or wasteful of energy, or likely to sap the nation's moral fibre.

The snowmobile was guilty on all three counts — or it wasn't, the viewpoint often depending on whether or not you'd ridden one. In 1969, back in the days when it was permissible to boast about squandering energy, the Canadian Snowmobile Association predicted that snowmobile owners, *in Quebec alone*, would burn up 14,250,000 gallons of gasoline in 1970. And in the machine's early days, before the spread of snowmobile clubs and the construction of designated snowmobile trails (there are now 13,000 miles of trails in Quebec alone), the propensity towards yahooism was immense. The sense of freedom which is the machine's chief psychic benefit encouraged too many riders to churn, uninvited, through countless farmers' fields, sometimes even cutting wire fences that impeded their progress. There were ugly stories of animals being chased to exhaustion by hunters on snowmobiles. The early machines were excessively noisy and, in inexperienced or irresponsible hands, they could be dangerous. Hundreds of people have lost their lives in snowmobile accidents, and Bombardier

Ltée remains extremely conscious of the latest body counts.

You could argue endlessly about whether this would be a better world if the snowmobile had never been invented. But your judgment is bound to be pretty subjective. Personally, I like to think that anyone who uses snowshoes or cross-country skis can be presumed to possess a more enlightened sense of life's rewards than someone who travels by snowmobile for fun. But I don't think you can legislate such enlightenment. Millions of people enjoy the things. Thousands of people depend on them. With every innovation, there's a time lag of a decade at least between its introduction and the legislative response to it. Once that response has been framed, and ways have been found to ensure that the snowmobile doesn't impinge on the use or enjoyment of the land by others, the controversy — which still renews itself every winter — will seem as quaint as the 1950s debates about television. ("I can contemplate a time," said Dr. Robert Maynard Hutchins, president of the University of Chicago in 1952, "when people can neither read nor write, but will be no better than the lower forms of plant life.") Some of the early predictions concerning the snowmobile's effects on the quality of life were almost as dire.

But that debate was still in the future when, in the early 1960s, the great snowmobile boom began. For almost a decade, Bombardier's sales more than doubled every year since the Ski-Doo's introduction. By the time of Joseph-Armand's death, Bombardier had sold more than 16,000 Ski-Doos and production continued to double annually for years after that. The company literally couldn't make them fast enough.

Other manufacturers got interested too, thus creating what almost amounts to a new class of snowmobile millionaires in Quebec. Rejean Houle, the 19-year-old son of a family that owned a small machine shop in Wickham, Quebec, built a few snowmobiles in 1963, and sold them under the name of Skiroule. Eight years later, the family sold the resultant company, now one of the industry's leaders, to the Coleman organization in an exchange of cash and shares which worked out to a price of about $18 million. In Thetford Mines, Quebec, four local businessmen, including a plumber, an accountant and a lawyer, combined in 1964 to build 25 snowmobiles under the brand-name Sno Jet. They eventually sold the company for $8 million. Another group of local entrepreneurs in La Pocatière, Quebec, launched a snow-mobile called Moto-Ski in 1963; like Bombardier, this company also got its start in a garage. When the founder, G. E. Bouchard, died five years later, the company was sold to a U.S. firm, Giffen Industries Inc. and, in 1971, was bought from Giffen by Bombardier.

U.S. manufacturers, most of them based in Minnesota and Illinois, got into the act too. Competing brands proliferated: Scorpion, Arctic Cat, Polaris, the Johnson Skee-Horse, Alouette, Sno-Prince, Starcraft.

The automobile industry, in its early days, spawned a horde of small firms, most of which were killed off or absorbed until the industry was dominated by a handful of giants. The snowmobile industry followed the same pattern. By 1968, there were more than 40 manufacturers in the field. A few years later there were more than 70. But some of them got in too late. Outboard Marine Corp., which started making snowmobiles around 1963, lost more than $30 million on the venture.

Bombardier survived and flourished for several reasons. For one thing, it was almost the first in the field, and its approach to the technology of snowmobiles was backed by several decades of experience in larger tracked vehicles. For another — and this was crucial — the company already had the nucleus of a dealer organization across North America. Unlike its competitors, most of whom had to tackle the distribution problem from scratch, the Ski-Doo came to Bombardier dealers as simply the latest in an array of products. Finally — and this may be the most decisive factor of all, even though it sounds almost ghoulish to say it — Joseph-Armand's untimely death (he was only 57) came at a timely moment in the company's development. The management team he'd arranged from his deathbed to succeed him was well equipped to carry the company from the status of an overgrown cottage industry to that of one of the country's major manufacturing concerns. Had Joseph-Armand lived, the company quite possibly would not have been as successful as it turned out to be. An unwritten law decrees that the man who starts a company is almost never equipped to carry it beyond a certain stage of growth. Joseph-Armand Bombardier, although he was one of Canada's great innovators, was not one of our great managers.

It was a money-losing sawmill, oddly, that led to the acquisition of the management skills the company needed. Joseph-Armand had lent money to a friend to start a sawmill near Megantic. It lost money consistently, and Joseph-Armand kept pumping in more cash. By 1962, the debt had grown to $150,000, and Bombardier's accountant in Montreal was advising him to shut the place down and write off his losses.

More or less by accident, Bombardier consulted two younger men about the matter: Charles Leblanc, then a young Sherbrooke lawyer whose father, also a lawyer, sometimes acted for Bombardier on family matters; and his own son-in-law, a 24-year-old chartered accountant named Laurent Beaudoin. Both advised him not to put the sawmill in bankruptcy. Instead, they arranged a transfer of ownership to Bombardier, and tried to find out what was wrong with the business.

It was a fairly routine exercise in business consultancy. They found two main problems: the mill had too many customers who didn't pay their bills; and it was cutting the wrong sizes of wood at the wrong times. In six months, Beaudoin and Leblanc turned it into a profitable company. Bombardier was impressed. He asked Leblanc and Beaudoin next to look into the matter of arranging his estate.

After studying the problem, they recommended that Bombardier buy out his three brothers, who then owned nearly 25 percent of the company. They also negotiated the purchase at a total price of about $1.8 million. "We thought this was a good price," Leblanc recalls, "but we knew how contrary the old man was. If we recommended he buy at that price, he'd be bound to turn it down. And so we recommended the opposite. We told him we thought the price was too high. Well, he raged at that. He said: to hell with it — I'll *give* the company to my brothers, and I'll start again in another garage, and I'll show them I can do it all over again!' But then he came around, just as we thought he would, and bought the shares."

Laurent Beaudoin had met his wife Claire when both were business administration students at the University of Sherbrooke. They married in 1959. Beaudoin had practised with a firm of chartered accountants in Sherbrooke for a year, then opened his own firm in Quebec City. He'd never been especially anxious to join his father-in-law's business. But the sawmill and estate transactions had involved him in the company's affairs. When Bombardier asked him to become comptroller, in May 1963, Beaudoin said yes.

In those first six months before Joseph-Armand contracted his fatal illness, Beaudoin almost quit in disgust several times. He'd been hired to handle the administrative end of the company, with Bombardier in overall command. "But I'm not sure how long I would have stayed," he recalled. "Mr. Bombardier was a very strong character. Everything had to go across his desk. Every time I made a decision, he'd ask me: 'Why did you do that?' I'd tell him, 'Well, that's what you hired me for.' "

"It was worse than that," recalls Leblanc. "Laurent used to come to me and say, 'He gives me authority one day, and takes it away the next!' I'd tell him: 'Hang on. If you quit, there'll be a real mess.' " Leblanc, by this time, was getting sucked into the organization too. Then, in the autumn of 1963, Joseph-Armand got sick, and it became impossible for them to leave.

Germain Bombardier, the eldest son, assumed the presidency after Joseph-Armand's death. There were tough decisions to be made, because almost uncontrollable growth was being forced upon the company. The demand for snowmobiles seemed almost limitless. The winter of Joseph-Armand's death, the company had sold 8,000 of them — and spent only $30,000 on advertising. Even that expenditure had been bitterly opposed by the founder. A good product, he told the young men who would soon succeed him, is its own best advertisement. Why spend money on intangibles?

But Bombardier's heirs recognized that his invention was more than a utilitarian replacement for dog teams and horse-drawn sleighs. It was, as a marketing man later described it, "an everybody product" — a new kind of recreational vehicle, which created a new kind of recreation. Selling snowmobiles would involve spending massive amounts on advertising to promote a new leisure-time activity, plus further investments in plant enlargement to meet the resultant demand. Using the company's substantial retained earnings, plus short-term borrowings from Banque Canadienne Nationale, Bombardier's new management jumped into a period of frantic expansion. In the 1964-65 season, it sold 13,000 Ski-Doos. The next year it was 22,000. Then 44,000. Then 71,000. For eight hyper-active years, Ski-Doo sales doubled, or more than doubled, every year.

"They didn't know how high was up," recalls John Hethrington, who was the company's marketing chief during the period of greatest expansion, "but they knew it was up. Remember, you had this $8 million company being run by a bunch of young kids, and *everybody* came to call, Outboard Marine, Chrysler, you name it. There were all kinds of companies that tried to buy Bombardier. Well, the tradition in Quebec is that you sell out to the Americans. So these guys had two choices: go clip coupons on the Riviera, or do it. They did it."

In the first two years of the new regime, *petites frictions* did develop, just as Joseph-Armand had predicted. Bombardier was now owned by a family holding company, in turn owned by Madame Bombardier; Germain; the three daughters, Claire (who'd married Laurent Beaudoin), Jeanine (who'd married Gaston Bissonette) and Huguette (who'd married an engineer named Jean-Louis Fontaine); and the youngest son, André, still in school.

As Joseph-Armand had explained to Leblanc before his death, he wanted disinterested outsiders — Leblanc and Jean-Paul Gagnon, who became financial vice-president — involved in the company as buffers between the family, who owned the shares, and Laurent Beaudoin and Germain Bombardier, who would run it. At times, it was a delicate straddling act. Some family members were wary of the pace of expansion Beaudoin wanted to impose. And Germain, as the company grew and the pressure increased, became less confident of his ability to manage. "His health wasn't too good from a nervous point of view," says one insider. Germain began spending more and more time away from the office and, late in 1965, decided to sell his shares to the other members of the family. Beaudoin was named president. He was 27. "I'm not a religious man," says Charles Leblanc, "but I sometimes think it must have been the hand of God that caused Bombardier's daughter to marry Laurent, and brought him into the company."

164

It may be a trifle excessive to attribute it to divine intervention, but the fact is that Beaudoin was the right man for the job of turning a small company into a very large one. He was energetic, he was ambitious and he was a team player. He possessed none of the technical genius that had been Bombardier's strongest asset, but he had a knack for hiring the right people. He was alarmingly young, but he grew with the job. Two other brothers-in-law, Jean-Louis Fontaine and Gaston Bissonnette, joined the company and grew with him. John Hethrington became vice-president of marketing in 1966. It was a small management group, and an inexperienced one. But by a process of frantic expansion, acquisitions of other companies and the building of a strong dealer organization, Bombardier managed to maintain its dominance of a highly competitive industry.

Two basic policies guided this expansion: vertical integration, and the decision to "go everywhere at once." Instead of aiming for dominance of a particular region, such as Quebec, Beaudoin's team decided in 1966 to compete vigorously wherever snowmobiles could be sold. They also decided to plow back their profits into the acquisition of suppliers. The company already owned Rockland Industries, which made rubber tracks; and Roski Ltd., in nearby Roxton Falls, which made fibreglass snowmobile parts. Between 1966 and 1971, Bombardier completed the process by acquiring Drummond Automatic Plating Inc., which galvanizes and chrome-plates bumpers and handlebars; La Salle Plastics Inc., of nearby Richmond, which makes plastic parts; Ville-Marie Upholstering Ltd., which makes snowmobile seats; Jarry Precision Ltd., which makes transmissions and other precision parts; and, in 1971, a competing company, Moto-Ski Ltd. In 1967, a Montreal sportswear manufacturer named Marvin Walker came to Bombardier with a great idea — the company should manufacture its own insulated snowmobile clothing. Bombardier bought a half-interest in Walker's companies, and later increased its interest to 90 percent.

The company's growth was symbolized by its taste in airplanes. They weren't an extravagance; most of Bombardier's business was in relatively inaccessible cities like Duluth, Minnesota, or Corner Brook, Newfoundland, or Pendleton, Oregon — places that took two or three connections to get to. Besides, if you bought them at year-end, as Bombardier did, you collected an immediate 30 percent tax write-off, and could usually resell the plane a year later for close to what you paid for it. Until 1967, the company had got along with a modest twin-engined Comanche. Then it was a Queen Air Twin, for $120,000; then a used Jet Commander for $600,000; then, in 1969, when Bombardier was doing business in Europe as well as across North America, a North American Sabreliner that cost $1.8 million.

It suited the company's high-flying style. By that time, in 1969, Bombardier was a public company. It sold 113,000 snowmobiles that year; net sales were $141.7 million, and the firm earned $16.8 million. The stock market favored them. At one point, the stock traded higher than $22, which meant the market valued the company at at least $320 million. As many as 4,000 employees worked in the new factory at Valcourt, and another 2,000 in Bombardier offices and subsidiaries elsewhere. It was a period of maximum cockiness. "Some economists," said the company in its 1970 annual report, "have referred to snowmobiles as riding the crest of the leisure market, but the wave shows no sign of cresting. All forecasts point to a positive and continuing upsweep of the trend well into the 21st century." There were hundreds of people at Bombardier, including many of the senior management, who seemed to believe the company could simply keep doubling production forever.

Contrary to "all forecasts," however, the wave began to crest about 1971. By now there were more than 100 competitors in the field, sales costs were rising, the economy was less buoyant and the market, it began to appear, was approaching saturation. The company had had too little time to think about the kind of diversification that would protect it from downturns in the snowmobile market. In the late 1960s, Bombardier introduced a California invention called the Sea-Doo — a water-borne snowmobile which used a two-cycle engine, and was propelled by jets of water. It was a disaster; the company lost between $2 million and $3 million on the Sea-Doo before dropping it. By the end of 1973, the stock was down to $2, earnings had dropped from $12 million to $547,000, 4,000 employees had been laid off. "They used to call me a hero," Beaudoin liked to say. "Now they call me a zero."

Early in 1974, Beaudoin dumped about 30 high-level executives, and merged Moto-Ski's marketing department with Bombardier's. It was a period of severe retrenchment, but Beaudoin seemed almost to welcome it. "There were so many empires getting built around here," says one executive, "and when sales and profits kept going up, there was no way to stop them. I think Laurent is actually enjoying it. It means he's recaptured a personal feel for the company."

It was Beaudoin, finally, who guided the company toward its next phase — that of an integrated transportation company. The oversold snowmobile market, plus the onset of the energy crisis, brought a disastrous downturn to the industry. "It forced us to diversify sooner than we thought," says Leblanc. The first major step in this direction was the awarding, in 1974, of a $116 million contract to build cars for the Montreal Metro. The plant in La Pocatière, Quebec, which once built Moto-Skis was modified to build the cars. And the Valcourt plant, the centre of the company's snowmobile manufacturing operations, was enlarged to build the wheeled trucks for the subway cars.

In 1975, Bombardier took another step: the acquisition, for $16 million of family money, of MLW Worthington Ltd., an American-controlled Montreal company that manufactures locomotives. In a move that seemed to symbolize a break with its origins, the company also shifted its head office to Montreal. There, a small management group which now includes Jean-Claude Hébert, a former Warnock Hersey executive who was brought in as board chairman, superintends an empire that still dominates the snowmobile market, but is now chiefly concerned with expanding into other fields of transportation.

The company not only had survived the death of its founder. It also had survived the collapse of the snowmobile boom it helped to create. It had traveled the whole route from the entrepreneurial innovative itch to corporate maturity. It had achieved the transition from a one-man company to a major industry — more or less as Joseph-Armand Bombardier had planned it on his deathbed.

APPENDIX

HOW TO ASK FOR
VENTURE CAPITAL

Varitech Investors Ltd. was an active, Toronto-based venture-capital firm during the late 1960s and early 1970s. The company's two principals, John Hardie and James McKinney, have since moved on to other areas of business, and Varitech no longer exists. But the brochure they prepared for prospective clients as an introduction to the venture-capital business, and to the process of asking venture-capital firms for money, is still the clearest, most concise presentation of the subject I've seen. And so, as a sort of how-to-do-it appendix, I'm reprinting it here.

Introduction

Venture capital is money which is provided to an enterprise to finance its development, in return for equity or partial ownership of the enterprise. The venture capitalist is the man or organization who provides the venture capital. To obtain venture capital, you must know what the venture capitalist wants and how he evaluates and monitors an investment.

When it comes to securing venture capital, there is no single formula which absolutely guarantees success. However, the method outlined here has worked very well in the past. If your proposition makes good financial sense and it is well-presented, then the method should also work for you.

I The venture capitalist

(a) Why does he do it?

First of all, the venture capitalist is not an ordinary investor, happy with safe returns and profits. He is not content with the interest rates readily available on commercial or government debt issues, the capital gains and income potential of real estate, or the obvious benefits of investment in listed public companies. Instead he is prepared to invest his money in high-risk ventures; with the expectation of commensurate rewards. The relationship of the risk and the reward governs the amount of equity (i.e. ownership) that a venture capitalist expects to acquire for his investment. If the risk is relatively low or the potential rewards are exceptionally high, the investor may settle for a smaller portion of the equity. Conversely he will expect substantially more equity in what he considers to be a very risky venture than he could obtain for the same money in a more secure investment.

(b) What the venture capitalist invests in

The venture capitalist usually prefers to invest in small enterprises with above-average chances of financial success. Typically, a business needs capital at three distinct stages in its evolution:

Stage I: Start-up

When capital is required to launch a new enterprise selling a promising product or new service in a well-researched market.

Stage II: Development

When an operational company with staff, plant and equipment and some customers, is finally about to realize or has just begun to realize its profit potential, and needs money to hang on until the profits actually arrive.

Stage III: Expansion

When a well-established, profitable company could benefit from substantial expansion but lacks the necessary extra funds.

170

Most venture capitalists prefer to invest in companies at the development or expansion stage because the future of the companies is more predictable. Some venture capitalists, however, will finance "start-ups" and "turn-arounds" as well, despite the added risks which are entailed. A "turn-around" is defined as a company that is in serious difficulty which can be re-established on a profitable basis by the injection of venture capital and new management.

(c) How the venture capitalist evaluates potential investments

Despite the best efforts of entrepreneurs and venture capitalists, a high percentage of emerging companies either get into serious difficulties or fail altogether. Perhaps the basic premise on which the enterprise was founded is wrong or ahead of its time; or the enterprise cannot adjust to unforeseen changes in the business climate or product technology. Other factors could be incompetent management or the inability to raise further capital when refinancing is necessary.

Because of these unpredictable factors, the venture capitalist will take every precaution before committing his funds to your enterprise. Generally, his attitude is to assume that what can go wrong will go wrong. So you must be prepared for the most detailed scrutiny of your proposal from every angle, and you should try to plan a course of action which anticipates all possible contingencies.

Many factors about your enterprise are important to the venture capitalist. He will judge your confidence in it by the extent to which you are willing to commit your personal assets and to live initially on a modest salary. He will be particularly interested in the projected profitability. However, the single factor on which he will ultimately base his decision to invest is the calibre of management. Each member of your management team must have unquestionable integrity and they must possess enough marketing, technical, financial and administrative expertise to attain corporate objectives. In addition, the team must be highly motivated to succeed, capable of working harmoniously under pressure and able to grow with the enterprise.

Many venture capitalists will overlook a shortcoming in your product or even your market. Few will compromise on the quality of your management.

(d) How the venture capitalist monitors an investment

After investing in a company, a venture capitalist will monitor his investment. Most want a seat on the board of directors; others prefer to work closely with the executive committee either as a member of the committee or as a consultant. Additionally, he will almost invariably insist on monthly reports. These will include all financial statements and may include general reports covering marketing, production, research and development, administration, and an up-dated summary of short- and long-range problems. He will probably insist that your financial forecasts be updated quarterly. While monitoring the progress of your enterprise, a venture capitalist can be of considerable value to you by bringing his management skills to bear on your corporate problems and by acting as a sounding board for your ideas.

II Four steps to obtaining venture capital

There are four steps to obtaining venture capital.
One, decide which venture capitalists to approach.
Two, decide when to approach them.
Three, decide how to approach them.
Four, decide how to negotiate with them.

1. Which venture capitalists to approach

Prior to 1968, only a handful of organizations offered venture capital to Canadian entrepreneurs; today there are at least two dozen. They will invest up to $1 million or more in enterprises which, after thorough investigation, appear to meet their requirements. They usually prefer situations which require in excess of $150,000 as any potential investment, regardless of its size, takes between four and six weeks to evaluate.

Some venture capital organizations also provide a wide range of managerial, financial and technical assistance. Therefore, you should find out which sources of venture capital have the resources that would be of most value to you. Most venture capitalists specialize in certain areas of business activity and tend to favor investment in those areas they know best. So find out what organizations are particularly interested in your type of enterprise.

From these factors, and any other information you may be able to pick up in the business community, you should determine which venture capitalists are your most likely prospects.

Of course, in certain cases, it may be advantageous to raise venture capital from a source other than an organization specializing in this type of financing. Occasionally, companies requiring less than $1 million can obtain venture capital by public financing. In addition, wealthy individuals and investment dealers are frequently sources of venture capital. However, these sources seldom offer any management assistance, and often are unwilling to provide secondary financing if it becomes necessary.

Another source of funds is the federal government which has a variety of aid and grant-giving programs for industry. However, these funds are not normally available until after equity financing has been completed.

2. When to approach venture capitalists

In seeking venture capital, it is extremely important that you select the right moment. If you approach your most likely sources before you are adequately prepared, you may ruin your chances of successfully obtaining funds from them. On the other hand, to wait too long may be equally damaging, for a shortage of cash can seriously interfere with the steady planned development of your enterprise. Also, the fact that you had not anticipated this in your planning can seriously undermine your credibility as a good manager. Remember, it will be at least six weeks after entering into negotiations before any funds become available.

There is no hard and fast rule as to when you should approach your selected sources. But there are three factors which will help you judge when the time is ripe. First, your enterprise must be developed as far as is possible within the limitations of your existing financial resources, to allow you to point to your accomplishments as a measure of the soundness of your ideas and your judgment. Second, you must have undertaken sufficient research and planning to prepare the detailed proposal discussed on the following pages. Third, and perhaps most important of all, you must be able to discuss your ideas lucidly and convincingly with potential investors and to communicate your own enthusiasm to them.

3. How to approach venture capitalists

When you decide it is time to look for venture capital and you have selected the most likely potential sources, your most crucial test begins. For venture capitalists will judge you not only on the validity of your ideas, but on the effectiveness of every aspect of your presentation. For this reason, it may be advantageous to try out your presentation on someone who you feel will offer objective criticism of your proposal such as your bank manager, lawyer or accountant. This will alert you to any weaknesses in your proposition and will allow you to sharpen your presentation. Then you will be prepared for future negotiations.

To make contact with venture capitalists in a manner likely to lead to negotiations, you need two tools: a brief one-page mini-proposal; and a comprehensive information brochure with complete supporting documentation.

The mini-proposal is a one-page summary which describes your enterprise, the market justification for it, its attractive features from an investor's point of view, and the amount of money you are attempting to raise.

Send the mini-proposal to a limited number of possible sources simultaneously. Then send a copy of the brochure to those who express interest. Do not distribute the brochure too widely if you can avoid it. Your ideas will seem shopworn if you start new negotiations and your brochure has been around for a few weeks. Furthermore, one venture capitalist will be hesitant to back an idea which he knows others have turned down. Other than your own personality, the brochure is the single most important selling tool that you have. It must be written in a simple straightforward manner; it must hold the reader's interest; and above all, it must be believable. Remember it will be thoroughly analyzed, and every omission will be noted. Keep the actual brochure as brief as is practical, but support its contents wherever possible with reference to third-party endorsements and independent evaluations which can be included in a back-up file. Remember, the more complete, concise and easy to understand the brochure is, the faster you will get a response. You will find that the following format is a good guide to developing your own brochure.

(a) Summary of contents — The summary can be the mini-proposal.

(b) History — Give a brief history of your enterprise describing when it was founded; by whom; and what has been achieved to date.

(c) The products (or services) — The existing or proposed products or services should be described in detail. Any patented or patentable features should be summarized. The customer benefits and economic advantages (if any) over existing competitive products or services must be outlined. Any sales literature, photographs, or drawings which help explain the product should be included in the back-up file.

(d) The market — Define the company's marketing philosophy. Outline a detailed marketing plan. Indicate the present and potential size of the total market and what market share you expect your product to obtain. Provide an analysis of competitors, including an evaluation of their products and pricing policies and an estimate of their market share. Note any special hazards or problems associated with the market. Name potential customers who have been contacted and who have shown enthusiasm for the product. Give the actual names of the people and their companies. Outline distribution and servicing facilities.

(e) Research and development — Describe any research and development projects that are contemplated, with the names of persons responsible. Include a timetable, the anticipated costs involved, and the expected results.

(f) Manufacturing plans — Give full details of the company's manufacturing facilities or proposed facilities. Outline the reasons for the choice of locations. Describe the size and cost of buildings. Describe the cost or anticipated cost of each major piece of equipment. Describe the production process. The costs of all facilities and equipment should be substantiated by invoices or third party quotations from prospective landlords, contractors, equipment suppliers, etc. In addition, the production process should be fully described and supported with diagrams. This material should be included in the back-up file.

(g) Management — Give a brief but complete résumé of all key personnel. Describe their exact responsibilities, areas of operation, salaries and equity participation.

(h) Cash flow and earnings projections — Accurate and detailed cash flow and earnings projections should be provided on a monthly basis for the first 24 months, and quarterly for the following three years. These estimates must be realistic. Thus, it may be advisable to prepare three separate forecasts: the most pessimistic, the most optimistic, and the most probable. All costs should be broken down into fixed and variable components. All assumptions reflected in the forecast should be explained fully by supporting material in the back-up file. Pro forma balance sheets and operating statements should be prepared for each of the five years. If audited financial statements for previous years are available these should be included together with the latest interim report.

(i) Financial requirements — Define precise capital needs of the company. This information should include the amount of money required, when it is required, and exactly how it will be used. All present shareholders should be listed, if possible. The number and class of shares owned, the amount paid for each share, and the dates on which they were purchased should be noted for each shareholder. Shareholders' loans or loans to shareholders should be noted. Disclose the type of deal you are looking for and how much equity you are prepared to sell to raise the necessary funds.

It is advisable to prepare personally as much of the brochure as is practical to ensure your own understanding of what it contains. However, you should use professional help in certain areas. In particular, you should enlist the services of a lawyer and a chartered accountant. Ask the chartered accountant for his comments and suggestions on the financial information. Ask the lawyer to ensure that legal considerations in the brochure are properly identified and dealt with.

Finally, make sure the brochure has an attractive, readable appearance. This will help make the information convincing and easily understood.

4. How to negotiate with venture capitalists

Negotiations with venture capitalists will provide an important opportunity to demonstrate your capabilities. Before negotiations begin, decide on the upper and lower levels of compromise that are acceptable to you. Be flexible. Offer the venture capitalist several options rather than a single choice. But also be firm, and indicate clearly that there are certain limits beyond which you will not proceed.

The venture capitalist is sizing you up during negotiations and you should take the opportunity to evaluate him. What are the managerial skills he can provide? Will he be easy to work with? What is his company like? Remember if your negotiations are successful, he is going to be your partner.

Don't be upset by the clinical approach taken by some professional investors. They do not have your personal commitment to your enterprise and view it strictly as a business proposition.

If the risk involved or the capital required dictates that the venture capital syndicate must have majority ownership, you should recognize that minority participation in a successful, dynamic enterprise is far more valuable than majority participation in a failure.

Conclusion

In summary, if your management team is competent and dedicated, your product or service marketable, your business plan well conceived, and your presentation convincing, you should be successful in securing the funds your enterprise requires.

The author,

Alexander Ross, came east from Vancouver
to Toronto, where he soon became one of the
best-known journalists in Canada. A former
managing editor of *Maclean's*, he has also
been a columnist for the *Toronto Star* and for
The Financial Post. He is now the editor of
Toronto Life.